Lorenzo Pradelli
Albert Wertheimer

Pharmacoeconomics

Principles and Practice

SEEd

© SEEd srl. All rights reserved
Piazza Carlo Emanuele II, 19 – 10123 Torino, Italy
Tel. 011.566.02.58 – Fax 011.518.68.92
www.edizioniseed.it
info@edizioniseed.it

First edition
December 2012

ISBN 978-88-9741-937-2

TABLE OF CONTENTS

PREFACE

Lorenzo Pradelli
AdRes Health Economics and Outcomes Research, Torino, Italy

Honestly, when I was first asked to serve as editor for a manual on pharmacoeconomics and outcomes research, my first thoughts were: "Another one? Are there not enough around?" and my skeptical face must have shown this, although I did answer that I would take a look on what was already available before making my decision. But then, as I actually did take a look around, I noticed that most of the literature is either academic in style (and weight!), or thought as a textbook for students, while not much is available for people who have to deal with economic evaluations in health care, but do not engage themselves in performing such studies.

So we decided to try and provide a text which can serve as a quick reference and as an aid to understand papers dealing with pharmacoeconomics and outcomes research, providing a slim basis of the theoretical background, but then exemplifying the concepts through examples taken from the literature, with the ambition to ease a sound acquaintance without the redundancy of technical details.

Accordingly, we structured the book in a first, short section in which the basic definitions commonly used in the jargon are provided, followed by a more in-depth exposition of the main methods and techniques, explained by the description of actual studies retrieved in the published literature.

The result is the present text, which the on-field experience of all involved authors has made, in our opinion, a practical tool that can guide stakeholders involved in the decision making process in health care to a robust insight of the theoretical and methodological aspects of modern pharmacoeconomics.

INTRODUCTION

Ceri J. Phillips
Swansea Centre for Health Economics,
College of Human and Health Sciences Swansea University

The assessment of pharmaceuticals has, in recent years, expanded beyond efficacy and safety to cover economic implications and other consequences. The incorporation of an economic perspective into the decision-making process as to which therapies will be reimbursed and made available by respective health care systems has aroused much debate and discussion, which at times has been quite heated. Newspaper headlines of people having to re-mortgage their houses to pay for "lifesaving" therapies and media frenzy when "effective" treatments are denied to desperate patients are becoming all too common occurrences. The intention of this introductory Chapter is to explore some of the concepts that underpin the economic assessment of pharmaceuticals in order to appreciate the rationale for economic considerations and how the approaches and instruments used in undertaking the economic assessments can be applied to everyday decision-making processes.

Health Care Dilemma

It cannot have escaped the attention of anyone involved in health services that there is a shortage of more or less everything that is needed to adequately provide services. The nature of the health care dilemma, which confronts all health care systems, is a microcosm of the basic economic problem: that of reconciling infinite wants, needs and demands with finite resource availability, in terms of income, time, expertise, and so on. The exponential increase in demand for health care services has been occurring at the same time as pressures on governments and funding agencies to carefully manage the volume of resources available for health care services. It is not simply a lack of finance – although that does feature prominently – but as individuals we are continually faced with the consequences of not having enough time to fit in everything that needs to be done and would very much like to do. In addition, shopping lists far exceed abilities to purchase everything they contain, while good intentions to maintain strict exercise routines are often thwarted by the lack of energy after a busy day at the office, in the surgery or in the operating theatre!

The fundamental economic problem is that while we all have unlimited wants and desires, we only have limited resources (time, energy, expertise and money) at our disposal to satisfy them. This situation has become particularly evident in health care and has been compounded by factors such as increasing expectations of people in relation to what can actually be delivered by health care services, continuing advancements in health technology and medical science and the increasing health needs and demands of an ageing population. As individuals we are constantly making choices as to how we use our time, into which activities we channel our energies and on what we spend our available funds. In spending time on one activity or purchasing a certain commodity, means that period of time and those funds are not available for other activities and other purchases. The same issues relate to health systems: which patients to treat, when and with what therapies? The answers do not lie in spending more money: how do we know whether any additional expenditure will actually produce additional health care benefits? Health care systems will never be a position to meet everyone's health care needs let alone people's wants and desires. The politicians, managers and other officials who run the services veer between trying to contain costs, and defusing the anger of patients, families and the electorate for the inadequacies in the services that are provided. Media focus on the pressures and problems, rather than the successes, do little to remedy the situation, while professionals' frustration and anger with what they see as the inadequacies in the systems and their effects on patient care are increasingly apparent.

▨ Opportunity Cost

It is therefore apparent that in making a choice to use funds and resources in one way means that they are not available for other purposes. As a result the benefits, which would have been derived, are sacrificed. These sacrifices are referred to as **opportunity cost**. Their very existence provide a rationale for economists to take an interest in all resources that are used, whether by individuals, governments, health services or societies, regardless of whether or not money is paid for them, in order to achieve the maximum benefit. Questions of resource allocation, that is how scarce resources are, could be or should be allocated amongst the infinite variety of competing activities, are therefore fundamental to any study of economics. The wide range of economic systems, which have existed and evolved over time, have all attempted to address the basic economic problem of allocating resources in such a way as to maximize the benefits for society. Similarly, the variety of approaches employed to fund and finance health care by different countries all have the same basic aim of seeking to maximize the health benefits for their citizens, given the resources they have available at that point of time. The nature, type and funding of health care systems continue to exercise the minds of many policy makers, and stimulate debate in academic institutions, the media and other popular centers of debate and discussion.

In developing a cost profile, it is important that the resource implications associated with the particular therapy being appraised in comparison with treatments that are currently provided should be identified, measured and valued within a relevant context and should include a comment on the validity of using resource data from other locations, if local data are not available. The appraisal should present direct health care resource usage for the therapy and its comparator(s) separately and in natural units, such as hospital days, dosage and duration of treatment, with data sources cited. These would constitute the costs to the respective health care system. However, patient resource use in accessing and using treatment should also be included where felt to be significant, particularly where there are major differences between the therapy and its comparator(s). Other resource use may also be presented separately where differences arise between the therapeutic agent and its comparator(s) e.g. direct non-health care resource use, such as those by other agencies, while productivity losses attributable to changes in health outcomes might also warrant some discussion.

Efficiency and Equity

The term **efficiency** is used by economists to consider the extent to which decisions relating to the allocation of limited resources maximize the benefits for society. The concept of efficiency embraces inputs (costs) and outputs and/or outcomes (benefits) and the relationship between them, with a society being judged in efficiency terms by the extent to which it maximizes the benefits for its population given the resources at its disposal. The simplest notion of efficiency is the one synonymous with economy, and is often referred to as **efficiency savings**, where output is expected to be maintained, while at the same time making cost reductions, or where additional output is generated with the same level of inputs. This type of efficiency has also been referred to as **cost-effectiveness**. It is applied where a choice needs to be made between alternatives, which seek to achieve the same goal, and exists when output is maximized for a given cost, or where the costs of producing a given output are minimized. It is widely used in the context where new therapies are compared against existing treatments and authorities have to decide whether it is worth paying more for the potential additional benefits which the new therapy offers.

10

However, cost-effectiveness is not sufficient in order to establish priorities, both within health care systems, and when comparing the provision of health care with other publicly funded services. In order to determine whether and how much of certain services should be provided and in order to establish priorities, allocative efficiency must be used. This type of efficiency exists when it is impossible to make one person better off without at the same time making someone else worse off. It represents a situation where no input and no output can be transferred so as to make someone better off without at the same time making someone else worse off.

However, it is impossible to separate the drive towards an efficient allocation of resources from its impact on income distribution. A move towards efficiency may well result in a redistribution of income in favour of the well off, which may not be acceptable on grounds of fairness and equity. Virtually all health care systems employ a mix of libertarian and egalitarian values. The notion of equity is inextricably linked with notions of fairness and justice, but it is important to distinguish it from the concept of equality. Policies designed to achieve equality of opportunity, or access, or utilization or outcome may well be desirous but they need not necessarily be equitable.

The extent of health inequalities within countries and across international boundaries continues to ensure that equity remains high on the list of health policy objectives. Many influential national and international policy documents highlight the importance of equity as a goal of policy and the on-going need to implement remedial measures to reduce inequalities both between and within populations, which remain frustratingly large. It is widely acknowledged that people's environment, social status, educational achievements, ethnic origin, age, gender, etc. affect their state of health, and equally that their conditions and characteristics result in some being better able to respond to treatments and enjoy longer life expectancy. An issue which has really polarized opinion, both within the health care professions and among decision-makers, for example, is whether people who knowingly engage in health-damaging behavior should receive treatment – is it fair and equitable that limited health care resources are allocated to these people, while others, who have attempted to live healthy lives, have to wait for treatment or access the services of the private sector? The very fact that service provision is limited makes it inevitable that some people will not receive all that is wanted or even required. The decision-making process as to who should receive services, treatments and interventions is littered with casualties, who can lay legitimate claim to claiming that such decisions are unfair and inequitable. In addition, there is a lack of consensus on how to deal with policies that improve efficiency while increasing inequalities or those that improve fairness while decreasing efficiency.

It is therefore very evident that in setting the economic objectives of health care systems, both efficiency and equity considerations are vital components and must be given serious consideration. However, it is inevitable that in seeking to achieve a more equitable allocation of resources, a level of efficiency will have to be sacrificed, or, in attempting to move to a more efficient health care system, inequalities in provision or access to services may have to be compromised.

Pharmacoeconomics

It is these issues that health economic evaluation seeks to address and, specifically in relation to pharmaceuticals, provides the underlying premise on which pharmacoeconomics is based. The term **pharmacoeconomics** has been coined to depict the economic assessment of pharmaceuticals, to assess the extent to which they provide additional benefits relative to the additional costs incurred. What is required is information that guides decision-makers as to which therapy provides the greatest bang per buck! In other words, is it worth paying more for the potential additional benefits which a new therapy offers when compared with existing treatments? The term **cost-effectiveness** has become synonymous with pharmacoeconomics and has been used (and misused) to depict the extent to which interventions measure up to what can be considered to represent value for money – what is the additional bang and what is the additional buck? Strictly speaking, however, cost-effectiveness analysis (CEA) is one of a number of techniques of economic evaluation, where the choice of technique depends on the nature of the benefits specified. CEA has been defined by NICE[1] as an economic study design in which consequences of different interventions are measured using a single outcome, usually in "natural" units (for example, life-years gained, deaths avoided, heart attacks avoided, or cases detected), and the interventions are compared in terms of cost per unit of effectiveness.

However, given that outputs and outcomes are highly specific and differ according to the nature of the condition, it is necessary to utilize "common currencies" so that apples and pears can be compared – that is outputs in obstetrics and gynecology need to be compared with outputs and outcomes in renal disease, care of the elderly, musculoskeletal disorders, etc. – so that the cost-effectiveness of an intervention in one therapeutic area can be compared with the cost-effectiveness of an intervention in a different area. The usual common currency that is employed is that of the quality adjusted life year (QALY), which is derived by the combination of the impact of the intervention on both quantity and quality of life. A QALY embraces both quantity and quality of life and is the arithmetic product of life expectancy and a measure of the quality of the remaining life-years. It provides a common currency for measuring the extent of health gain that results from health care interventions and, when combined with the costs associated with the interventions, can be used to assess their relative worth from an economic perspective. The quantity of life, expressed in terms of survival or life expectancy, is a traditional measure that is widely accepted and has few problems of comparison – people are either alive or not. Quality of life, on the other hand, embraces a whole range of different facets of people's lives, not just their health

---

[1]   http://www.nice.org.uk/media/B52/A7/TAMethodsGuideUpdatedJune2008.pdf

status. Even restricting the focus to a person's health-related quality of life will result in a number of dimensions relating to both physical and mental capacity. A number of approaches have been used to generate these quality of life valuations, referred to as health utilities: for example, standard gamble, time trade-off and the use of rating scales. The utilities that are produced represent the valuations attached to each health state on a continuum between 0 and 1, where 0 is equivalent to being dead and 1 represents the best possible health state, although some health states are regarded as being worse than death and have negative valuations. The specific type of cost-effectiveness analysis that is undertaken when using QALYs is referred to as cost-utility analysis (CUA).

There may be occasions when the outcomes generated by interventions are virtually equal or at least very similar. In such circumstances it might be possible for a cost-minimization analysis (CMA) to be undertaken, where only the cost differences between the interventions are needed to establish which of them provides the best value for money. However, caution should be exercised in relation to what is meant by equivalence or similarity – the condition for use of CMA is that the outcomes should be identical – since while both oral and IV modes of a drug can provide equivalent therapeutic outcomes, the outcomes from a patient's perspective can be very different.

In cost-benefit analysis (CBA) the costs and outcomes are expressed in monetary terms, so as well as being able to make comparisons across all areas of health care, comparisons can also be made with programmes and schemes in education, transport and the environment, for example. The difficulty arises, however, when trying to place a monetary value on the intangible benefits, where market prices do not exist. There are two main techniques that can be used here: these are willingness- to-pay and discrete choice experiments.

What is important to bear in mind is that the aim of all approaches used to undertake pharmacoeconomic assessments is to maximize the level of benefits – health effects – relative to the level of resources available. However, the complexities and

14

contentions relating to the assignment of monetary valuations to health care outcomes and the inadequacies of CEA and CMA has mean that CUA has become the primary technique used in conducting pharmaceconomic evaluations.

Further discussion on these approaches forms the basis of the remainder of this book.

▨▨▨▨ Sensitivity Analysis

Pharmacoeconomics is far from being a precise science and the findings emerging from such evaluations should be treated with a degree of caution. There is often considerable uncertainty associated with the findings with wide variation surrounding the results generated and it is therefore imperative that all phar-macoeconomic assessments should be subjected to a sensitiv-ity analysis. The need for sensitivity analysis arises because of a number of factors:

* methodological issues arising from different approaches and methods employed in the evaluation;

* potential variation in the estimates of costs and effects used in the evaluation;

* extrapolation from observed events over time or from intermediate to final health outcomes;

* transferability of results and the validity of results from different populations/patient groups.

The findings from cost-effectiveness assessments therefore re-quire some indication of the confidence that can be placed in them. What would happen, for example, if the "true cost" of one of the treatment strategies was somewhat higher or lower than the estimate used in the investigation or if there were signifi-cant changes in the life-years gained or other parameters used? Sensitivity analysis tests all the assumptions used in the model and enables the impact of changes on the baseline estimates. More information on sensitivity analysis will be provided later in the book.

▨▨▨ Summary

The decision-making process in determining which services and treatments should be provided is highly complex and involves a number of different, often conflicting, factors. The utilization of pharmacoeconomics can assist decision makers to utilise the information relating to the effectiveness and efficiency of an intervention. They can also go some way to contributing to the process of determining health care priorities and in seeking to ensure that the most efficient use is made of resources available within limited health care budgets. Health care professionals are increasingly being exposed to extremely powerful and emotive choices, and in no way can pharmacoeconomics provide the solution to such complex and difficult issues. What it does offer is a mode of thinking which can assist in arriving at possible solutions (notice the use of the term "assist" here – pharmacoeconomics cannot by itself offer the solutions, it has to be part of a wide-ranging approach to decision-making) to these often contentious problems. It aims at identifying which therapies would provide the maximum health care benefit for society within the envelope of resources available. It is the same process as we go through as individuals, in making that decision between a holiday abroad or a new kitchen – the one will provide us with significant benefits within a short period of time but the duration of these will soon diminish as we return to our normal existence.

The kitchen, on the other hand, will provide fewer benefits immediately in comparison, but the duration of the benefits will extend for a number of years. The prices of the alternatives are basically the same but we can only afford one of them. What factors should be considered in making the decision? How should these difficult choices be made? How should it be decided which therapies to fund? The use of pharmacoeconomics techniques can help in making these decisions but they should always be just one part of a multi-faceted process, with other factors also being considered.

16

Further Readings

* Drummond MF, Sculpher MJ, Torrance GW, et al. Methods for the economic evaluation of health care programmes. Oxford: Oxford University Press, 2005
* Phillips CJ. Health economics: an introduction for health professionals. Oxford: Blackwell Publishing, 2005

DEFINITIONS AND BASIC CONCEPTS

Albert Wertheimer
PhD, MBA. Professor of Pharmacy,
Department of Pharmacy Practice, Philadelphia

1.1 Definitions

Pharmacoeconomics arises from a fusion of pharmacy and economics. Economics is defined as «a social science concerned chiefly with description and analysis of the production, distribution, and consumption of goods and services» [Merriam-Webster's Collegiate Dictionary, Tenth Edition].

In pharmacoeconomics the "goods and services" are pharmaceutical products and services, and it is the effects of their consumption that is the focus of interest. Thus, we may define pharmacoeconomics as a social science concerned with the description and analysis of the costs of pharmaceutical products and services and their impact on individuals, health care systems, and society. Pharmacoeconomics is a subset of health economics, which deals with health care services in general rather than being restricted specifically to pharmaceuticals.

Because pharmacoeconomics is a social science substantially concerned with events in clinical practice, it overlaps with a branch of medicine called "outcomes research". Outcomes research is the study of the clinical (e.g., presence of disease), economic, or humanistic (e.g., patient quality of life) end results ("outcomes") of providing health care services. Pharmacoeconomics is that subset of outcomes research that deals with pharmaceuticals and includes economic outcomes.

1.2 Costs

The definitions of some cost terms commonly used in pharma-coeconomics are given in Table I.

First of all, economists distinguish **average cost** from **marginal cost**.

In practice the marginal cost is usually greater than the average cost.

Average costs can be then distinguished from **incremental costs**. The incremental cost is the increased cost of one health care program relative to an alternative. The incremental cost differs from the marginal cost in that the former relates to treatment alternatives while the latter refers to more of the same treatment.

Term	Definition
Average cost	Total cost divided by the number of units produced
Direct cost	The cost of the goods and services that are used in providing a treatment
Incremental cost	The increased cost of one treatment program relative to an alternative
Indirect cost	The value of the productivity loss resulting from an illness
Intangible cost	The value of psychosocial effects such as pain and suffering
Marginal cost	Change in total cost that results from the production of an additional unit
Mortality cost	The cost incurred due to death
Opportunity cost	The value of all costs in an alternative use
Overhead cost	The cost of providing space, power, administrative services, etc.
Production cost	The total amount of resources used in producing something
Productivity cost	Same as indirect cost

Table I. Definitions of pharmacoeconomic costs.

The distinction between **direct** and **indirect costs** is particularly relevant to cost-of-illness analysis. The direct cost of an illness, such as asthma, to society is the cost of providing all of the health care services to treat it, including the costs of medicines, physician visits, emergency room visits, and hospitalizations due to asthma. The indirect cost to society is the value of the productivity lost when asthma prevents people from working. Most direct costs considered in pharmacoeconomic analysis are direct medical costs, i.e., the costs of physician visits, hospitalizations, laboratory tests, drugs, and medical supplies and equipment. Non-medical costs include a variety of out of-pocket expenses, such as transportation to health care facilities, special foods, etc.

Direct costs = Direct medical costs + Direct non-medical costs

Indirect costs, i.e., productivity costs, arise from morbidity – when people miss work (absenteeism) or are less productive while at work (presenteeism) – and mortality.

Indirect costs = Morbidity costs + Mortality costs

In computing total costs, researchers may include not only the direct and indirect costs but also **intangible costs**. Intangible costs include the value placed on pain and suffering.

Total costs = Direct costs + Indirect costs + Intangible costs

1.3 Consequences

1.3.1 | Economic Outcomes

The word "cost" is taken to mean two different things in a pharmacoeconomic analysis, i.e., the non-monetary costs, referring to the health care and other resources consumed, and the monetary value of these resources.

Monetary Costs

The true monetary costs of the health care resources used are not necessarily easy to determine and in practice several surrogate measures are used. Charges by providers may be equated with cost. However, these charges are not necessarily the same as the true cost to the provider nor equivalent to the payments they actually receive. The cost of medical services and pharmaceuticals can be equated with the actual reimbursements that the health care insurer paid to the provider. List prices for drugs and fee schedules for medical services are available.

Non-monetary Costs

Direct non monetary costs are expressed as the health care resources consumed by a program or treatment alternative. These typically are the costs of physician visits, hospitalizations, laboratory tests, drugs, and medical supplies. The numbers of these events are counted. The indirect costs may be expressed in terms of the number of work-loss days, or the number of days off school.

1.3.2 | Patient Outcomes

Physiological

Patient outcomes may be expressed in terms of a physiological variable such as blood pressure, bone mineral density, or serum concentration of cholesterol, etc. In a cost-effectiveness analysis of a cholesterol-lowering drug, for example, the patient endpoint might be the average percentage reduction in serum cholesterol concentration. These kinds of variables can

22

be measured objectively using medical instrumentation. However, such "hard" endpoints are criticized as not being directly experienced by patients and thus not directly relevant to patients' feelings of well-being.

Mortality and Morbidity

In between the objective physiological endpoints and subjective humanistic endpoints are mortality and morbidity. Death is both relevant to patients' lives and objectively measurable. Morbidity – a diagnosis, e.g., heart failure, or pneumonia, and the effects on the patient's ability to function – is also relevant to patients' lives and may be based at least in part on objective data. Diagnoses, however, are usually based in part on patients' symptoms, which are by definition subjective.

Humanistic

In outcomes research, endpoints more directly relevant to patients' experience of their lives are often chosen. These "humanistic" endpoints include quality of life and patient satisfaction. While more relevant to patients' expressed desires, humanistic endpoints are based on patients' perceptions of their lives and are by definition subjective.

Quality of Life

The measurement of quality of life is an attempt to measure the totality of a person's experience of life, including work, recreation, social activities, sex life, etc. In pharmacoeconomics, we are usually interested in the impact of a person's health status on their quality of life, i.e., their health-related quality of life. Standardized questionnaires measure either health-related quality of life in general or quality of life in the context of a specific disease. The Medical Outcomes Study Short Form 36, or SF36, is a widely used generic health-related quality-of-life instrument. The SF36 has eight domains, including physical functioning, social functioning, role functioning, psychological distress, general health perceptions, bodily pain, vitality, and psychological well-being. An example of a disease-specific questionnaire is a migraine quality-of-life questionnaire that measures migraine symptoms, work functioning, social functioning, vitality, and the migraine sufferer's feelings or concerns about her or his migraine and its treatment [Hartmaier, 1995].

Patient Preference and Satisfaction

The same psychometric techniques that are used to measure quality of life can be applied to patients' satisfaction with the health care they receive. Patients might be asked to rate the health care provider's knowledge and skill, the quality of the interpersonal care, their degree of trust in the provider, etc.

1.4 Perspectives

Since costs are seen differently from different points of view, the perspective of any pharmacoeconomic analysis must be explicitly stated. Society, health care insurers (payers), and health care providers all have different perspectives on costs. Furthermore, the organization of health care financing, and therefore the appropriate cost perspective, varies from country to country and within countries such as the United States that have mixed systems. The usual perspectives in cost-effectiveness analysis are those of society and those of the program.

Example

A science writer with coronary heart disease is hospitalized following an acute myocardial infarction that subsequently proves fatal. From the perspective of the science writer's health care insurer (the payer), the cost of hospitalization is the amount of money paid to the hospital under the terms of the health plan. From the perspective of the provider (the hospital), the cost is the true cost of providing the hospital services. From the perspective of the science writer's employer, which (in this fictional example) entirely subsidizes its employees' health plans, the cost is that part of the insurance premium designed to cover coronary heart disease, plus the indirect costs, i.e., the cost of the productivity lost while the science writer was incapacitated, and the cost of hiring a replacement.

1.5 ▓▓ Time Horizon

The term "time horizon" is used to specify a period of time during which the outcomes of an analysis will be considered. The
time horizon could be expressed as a fixed number of years (or
months or weeks) or relative to study variables (e.g., patients'
lifetimes, or the amount of time that patients were enrolled in
a clinical trial). More precisely, the time horizon is a point in the
future up to which all costs and effects must be accounted for
and beyond which everything can be ignored.

Example

A cost-effectiveness analysis of the ACE-inhibitor enalapril based
on data from the SOLVD trial considered two time horizons:
a within-trial horizon, and a patients' lifetimes horizon [Glick,
1995]. The within-trial horizon referred to the actual time
period of the SOLVD trial. Because of staggered enrolment
and deaths during the trial, the durations of enrolment varied
up to the maximum duration of the trial (about five years). The
within-trial analysis relied on observed data of the effectiveness
of enalapril (cost data were inferred). The lifetime analysis was
a projection of events into the future.

1.5.1 Discounting

If the time horizon of a pharmacoeconomic analysis is several
weeks or months, no adjustment for changes in costs over time
is required. If the time horizon is several years, however, then
costs that are incurred at different times must be brought to
same reference time point.

The value of a dollar today is not what it was, say, twenty years
ago. For example, the cost of a drug in 2012 must be expressed
in dollars for the current year (or the reference year of the analysis) by increasing it according to the annual inflation rate for
pharmaceuticals. Conversely, the value of a dollar twenty years

from now will be less than its **present value**. In order to bring future costs to the same frame of reference as present costs, they must be discounted.

Example

The cost of a medical service is $1,000. The medical service will be utilized five years from now: what is its present value? The formula for discounting prices into the future is:

$$C_{present} = \frac{C_n}{(1+r)^n}$$

where $C_{present}$ is the current cost, n is the number of years, C_n is the cost n years from now, and r is the discount rate. If the discount rate is 5% per annum, the present cost of the medical service is:

$$C_{present} = \frac{1,000}{(1+0.05)^5} = \$784$$

---

2 PHARMACOECONOMIC EVALUATIONS

Albert Wertheimer
PhD, MBA. Professor of Pharmacy,
Department of Pharmacy Practice, Philadelphia

2.1 Introduction

There are essentially two kinds of health economic analyses: cost analysis and cost-outcomes (or cost-consequence) analysis.

In cost analysis, only the costs of providing health care products or services are considered, without regard to the outcomes experienced by the patient or providers. In a cost outcomes analysis, the endpoint of the analysis is a ratio of the costs of providing health care and a measure of the outcomes of the care. The main types of analysis are listed in Table II.

Method of analysis	Cost measure	Outcome measure
Cost analysis		
Cost of care	Currency	N/A
Cost-outcomes analysis		
Cost-effectiveness	Currency	Natural units, e.g. life years saved
Cost-utility	Currency	Quality-adjusted life years or other utility
Cost-benefit	Currency	Currency
Cost-minimization	Currency	Natural units or utilities

Table II. Common pharmacoeconomic analyses and methodologies.

2.2   Cost Analysis

2.2.1   Cost of Care

A cost of care analysis is an enumeration of the health care resources consumed – in this case drugs, pharmacy services, etc. – and the dollar costs of providing care to a given patient population over a given time period. The outcomes resulting from the care are not considered.

2.2.2   Cost of Illness and Burden of Illness

A cost of illness analysis normally falls under the umbrella of outcomes research rather than of pharmacoeconomics. In classical cost of illness analysis, the total cost that a particular disease imposes on society is expressed as a single dollar amount. Included in the calculation might be the costs of providing care for the illness (including drug therapy), the value of the lost productivity, and the monetary cost to society of premature death. Classical cost of illness analysis has metamorphosed in recent years into the burden of illness analysis, which in essence is the same thing except that the emphasis is placed on the more tangible component costs rather than on an aggregate dollar figure. Thus, the total direct medical costs of treating an illness, the number of deaths, hospitalizations, lost work days, etc., are the variables of interest in a burden of illness analysis. The most infamous misuse of cost of illness and burden of illness analysis is to be found in the opening paragraph of many a medical economic article, where future projections of the societal impact of the disease in question are delivered for their rhetorical effect.

2.3   Cost-outcomes Analysis

The different methodologies for cost-outcomes analysis are essentially similar in that the endpoint is a ratio of the costs and outcomes; they differ in the way the outcomes are expressed (Table II).

28

2.3.1 | Cost-effectiveness

Cost-effectiveness analysis (CEA) compares two (or more) alternative treatments for a given condition in terms of their monetary costs per unit of effectiveness. The unit of effectiveness can be any "natural" unit – e.g., percent lowering of LDL-C, major coronary events, number of lives saved, or years of life saved. The units of cost (currency and year) and effectiveness must be the same for the treatments compared. Cost-effectiveness analysis is used to decide among two or more treatment options. The definition of "cost-effectiveness" is discussed in more detail below.

The cost-effectiveness ratio may be given as a single number, but it may be more illuminating to present cost-effectiveness data graphically as a plot of costs versus effects.

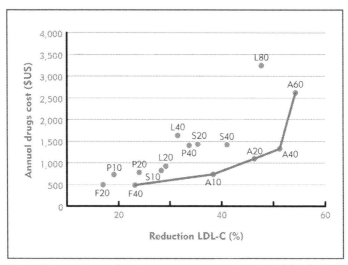

Figure 1. Annual cost of statins versus percent reduction in LDL-C. Scatter plot using data of Hilleman et al. [Hilleman, 2000]. The line connects drugs and dosages that lie on the "efficient frontier" of least cost for any degree of effectiveness.

A = atorvastatin (A10 = atorvastatin 10 mg, etc.); F = fluvastatin; L = lovastatin; S = simvastatin; P = pravastatin

Figure 1 shows a plot of the costs of treating hypercholesterolemia with statins (i.e., the drug costs) versus the effects of statin treatment (expressed as percent reduction in LDL-C). The points represent different statins and different dosages. The line connecting those points representing the lowest cost at any given effectiveness describes the "**efficient frontier**". In Figure 1, fluvastatin and atorvastatin are the only two statins on the efficient frontier – fluvastatin at lesser and atorvastatin at greater effectiveness.

Decision Analysis

Decision analysis provides the basic framework for cost effectiveness analysis, which is the most common type of pharmacoeconomic analysis. Decision analysis is a systematic, quantitative approach to assessing the relative value of one or more alternatives.

The basis of decision analysis is the decision tree. Figure 2 illustrates the components of a decision tree: nodes (decision, chance, and terminal) and branches. A series of chance nodes and branches connect a decision node with terminal nodes, which represent the outcomes of interest in the analysis. The tree is structured from left to right. The tree in Figure 2 begins with a decision node and two branches representing alternative

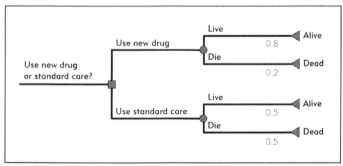

Figure 2. Hypothetical decision tree. The tree consists of branches (lines) and nodes: a decision node (square), chance nodes (circular), and terminal nodes (triangular).

2. Pharmacoeconomic Evaluations

courses of action, i.e., to use either a new drug or standard care to treat disease X. Both courses lead to a chance node that diverges into branches representing the possible outcomes of survival or death following treatment. These branches end in terminal nodes, representing the outcomes of interest in this decision analysis, i.e., life or death. Chance nodes identify points at which two (or more) possible events may occur. Which event will occur cannot be predicted with certainty, and so the chance nodes are associated with a probability for each emergent branch.

In this case, the probability of survival following treatment with the new drug is 0.8 and the probability of death is 0.2; these probabilities must sum to unity and the branches exiting the chance node must exhaust the possible outcomes. Following standard care, the probabilities of surviving and dying are both 0.5.

In this explanatory example, it is easy to see that the new drug is superior to standard care in terms of the number of surviving patients.

Definition of Cost-effectiveness

Decision trees such as the hypothetical example shown in Figure 2 are a basic step in cost-effectiveness analysis. Suppose that in the example shown in Figure 2 the cost of providing the new drug therapy to 100 patients was $1,000.

This includes the cost of the new drug and the cost the physician's services for diagnosing the condition and prescribing the treatment. Since 80 of the 100 patients given the new drug lived, the cost-effectiveness ratio is $1,000 divided by 80, or $12.5 per life saved. This ratio is referred to as the average cost-effectiveness ratio.

The cost-effectiveness ratio of interest is not the average cost-effectiveness ratio but the incremental cost-effectiveness ratio of the new drug relative to standard care. Suppose that, in the example shown in Figure 2, the cost of providing standard care to 100 patients was $300. Standard care is thus less costly than the new drug, but also less effective. The incremental cost-effectiveness of the new drug relative to standard care is the difference in costs divided by the difference in effects.

$$C/E = \frac{C_a - C_b}{E_a - E_b}$$

In this case, the difference in costs is $1,000 minus $ 300, or $ 700, and the difference in effects is 80 minus 50 lives, or 30 lives. The incremental cost-effectiveness ratio is thus $700 divided by 30, or $23.33 per life saved.

The incremental cost-effectiveness, and not the average cost effectiveness, is calculated because there is always an alternative to the new drug or whatever therapy is in question. Even if the alternative is literally to do nothing, there are associated costs and/or effects. Suppose that, in the example we are discussing, if literally nothing is done to treat 100 patients with disease X, then 70 patients die and 30 spontaneously recover and survive. There are no associated medical costs because no treatment is provided. This is illustrated in Figure 3.

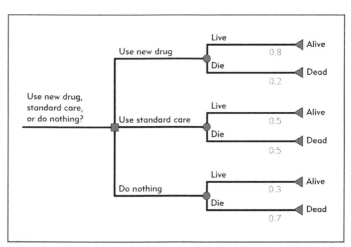

Figure 3. Hypothetical decision tree with three alternatives. Even if the alternative is literally to do nothing, the outcomes of interest accrue.

The incremental cost-effectiveness of the new drug relative to no treatment is:

$$\frac{\$1,000 - \$0}{80 - 30} = \$20.00 \text{ per life saved}$$

Similarly, the incremental cost-effectiveness of standard therapy relative to no treatment is $15.00 per life saved. Relative to no treatment, the standard therapy for disease X is less effective but more cost-effective than the new drug.

2.3.2 Cost-utility

A cost-utility analysis (CUA) is performed in the same way as a cost effectiveness analysis except that the unit of effectiveness is quality-adjusted life years (QALYs) or another measure of utility. Consider that the outcome of a treatment may be a prolonged life but with a degree of disability, or a reduced probability of disability without prolongation of life. The value or "utility" that individuals or society place on different life outcomes can be quantified using a number of techniques.

Since the endpoint is in practice always expressed as cost per quality-adjusted life-year saved, cost-utility analysis can, in principle, be used to compare not just alternative therapies for the same disease but therapies for different diseases, and rankings of the cost-utilities can be drawn up. Such rankings can be useful in selecting policies when, for example, a government wants to choose among installing highway guard rails, hiring additional food inspectors, or vaccinating seniors for flu.

An example of cost-utility analysis is provided in Chapter 3.

2.3.3 Cost-minimization

A cost-minimization analysis is a cost-effectiveness analysis in the special case in which the effectiveness of the treatments is the same. Once the effectiveness (expressed in whatever natural units are appropriate) has been determined to be equivalent for the alternative treatments, it is not considered further and the analysis focuses entirely on the costs, with the aim of determining which treatment minimizes costs. A cost-minimization analysis is, in effect, a cost-of care analysis in which alternative treatments are compared. Unlike a true cost-of-care analysis, however, the outcomes are taken into account and must be shown to be equivalent.

2.3.4 | Cost-benefit

Like cost-effectiveness analysis, cost-benefit analysis compares the costs and outcomes of alternative therapies; unlike cost-effectiveness analysis, however, the outcomes in a cost-benefit analysis are expressed in monetary terms. For example, the outcome of the treatment in question is first expressed in terms of life-years saved or quality-adjusted life-years saved, and this is then translated into an equivalent monetary amount-under the human capital approach, this amount is the present value of a person's lifetime productivity. Since both the costs and the effects of the treatment are expressed in the same (monetary) units, they can be directly compared. Any cost-benefit ratio of less than 1.0 is cost-beneficial. A ratio of 1:6 means that one receives $6 of value for $1 of investment.

2.4 Utility

The effectiveness of many medical treatments can be expressed in terms of prolongation of life, e.g., as the (average) number of years of life saved. Some treatments, however, may prevent a worsening in the quality of life without actually extending it. Similarly, a treatment may extend life but with the presence of significant disability that reduces the quality of life. These situations are dealt with by placing a value on the quality of life, i.e., its utility.

The utility of normal health is given a value of 1, while the utility of not being alive is set at 0; a state of reduced health has a value between 0 and 1. This utility (U) is multiplied by the number of years of life (Y) associated to the treatment in order to arrive at the number of quality-adjusted life years (QALYs):

$$QALY = Y \times U$$

QALYs are very suitable as measure of health outcome since they simultaneously capture gains from reduced morbidity (quality gains) and reduced mortality (quantity gains). Figure 4 displays individual's health-related quality of life deterioration with and without intervention. QALY gained is represented by the gray area between the two curves that can be divided into two parts: area A is the amount of QALY gained due to quality improvement and area B is the amount of QALY gained due to quantity improvement.

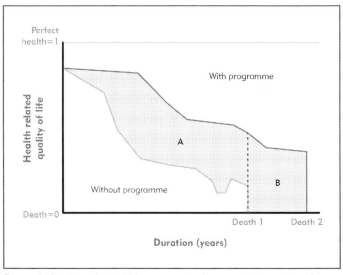

Figure 4. Quality-adjusted life years gained from an intervention [Drummond, 1997]. Gray area represents QALY gained: area A is the gain in health-relared quality of life during the time that the person would have otherwise been alive anyhow while area B is the amount of life extension, factored by the quality of life extension.

A related concept is the disability-adjusted life year (DALY). The DALY was developed to quantify the burden of disease and injury on societies (as in the Global Burden of Disease Study [Murray, 1997]) and represents the reduction in the number of years of life due to disease, weighted by the quality of life due to the presence of the disease. The DALY is obtained from the sum of two components: year of life lost (YLL) and years lived with disability (YLD) at the population level, hence reflects the burden of disease in the population [La Torre, 2010].

2.5 Psychometrics

The measurement of humanistic endpoints, such as quality of life, in medicine is based on questionnaires (see also Chapter 5). While a simple questionnaire might collect descriptive data such as the respondent's gender, favourite colour, etc., the questionnaires used in the health sciences are grounded in psychometric theory and are used to quantify various dimensions of health; they are referred to as "instruments".

The elements of an "instrument" are listed in Table III.

The typical instrument consists of a set of scales or "domains". A domain is designed to measure a particular "construct" or concept, such as social functioning or mental health. Each domain

Element	Description
Item	A single question or statement paired with its response options
Domain (dimension)	A concept measured by a group of items
Scale	Items representing domains combined to produce a score
Profile	Several different domains displayed as separate scores
Index	An aggregate score of several domains
Battery	Several instruments combined to provide a comprehensive understanding of a disease or intervention

Table III. The elements of questionnaires [Anonymous, 1996].

typically consists of several questions (or "items"), each item relating to a slightly different aspect of the construct. The options for response to each item might be a simple yes or no. These responses might be scored as 1 or 0 and an average score for the responses to all the items in the domain can be computed. A more sensitive way to structure the responses is to provide more than two options. For example, the items could be phrased as statements and the response options could be the following: strongly agree, agree, neutral, disagree, or strongly disagree. The domains in Examples 1 and 2 are "scales", because they generate a range of scores that measure the constructs represented by the domains. We have discussed multi-item scales, but a scale (or domain) might also contain only a single item. In the world of health-related questionnaires, psychometric instruments are not simply designed and used: they must be subjected to a series of tests to determine their reliability and validity. First, it is necessary to determine whether the different items in a scale reliably measure a common construct. This measure of reliability is called internal consistency. Internal

---

Example 1

A domain in an instrument contains three items, each with the response options of yes or no, scored as 1 or 0, respectively. The maximum score for the domain is 3 and the minimum score 0. Intermediate scores of 1 or 2 are possible. These five response options could be scored, for example, 4, 3, 2, 1, and 0, respectively. Items with the responses structured in this way are known as Likert scale.

Example 2

A domain in an instrument contains three items, each with the response options structured as Likert scales with five options, scored from 0 to 4. The maximum score for the domain is 12 and the minimum score 0. Intermediate scores from 1 to 11 are possible.

consistency is computed by calculating an aggregate of the correlations among the different items of the scale.

Another common test of reliability is called test-retest reliability. It measures the extent to which the answers are the same when the questionnaire is given to the same people on two different (but closely spaced) occasions. If the scores on the instrument are very different on the two occasions, the wording of the questions should be re-examined.

In addition to reliability, the validity of the instrument should be assessed. The distinction between reliability and validity can be seen if we think about the analogy of measuring skull diameter in order to assess intelligence. We could measure skull diameter using a variety of different methods that might vary in their accuracy and reproducibility, such as a visual assessment, a tape measure, or a CAT scan: these methods vary in their reliability. No matter how reliable the measurement method, however, the skull diameter is not a valid way of estimating human intelligence because there is no demonstrable relationship between the two. There are various approaches to the validity of psychometric instruments. One common measure, construct validity, assesses the relationship between the instrument and the construct it is designed to measure. Construct validity is determined by comparing instrument scores with some other measure of the construct.

3 MODELING FRAMEWORKS

Albert Wertheimer
PhD, MBA. Professor of Pharmacy,
Department of Pharmacy Practice, Philadelphia

Lorenzo Pradelli
AdRes Health Economics and Outcomes Research, Torino, Italy

3.1 Steps in Decision Analysis

While the process may be broken down in a number of different ways, we will follow previous authors and describe a decision analysis in terms of five steps [Petitti, 1994]:

* identify and bound the problem;
* construct the decision tree;
* collect the information to fill the decision tree;
* analyze the decision tree;
* conduct a sensitivity analysis.

3.1.1 Example: Emergency Contraception and Pregnancy

National survey data for 1994 indicate that 49% of all pregnancies were unintended; 54% of the unintended pregnancies ended in abortion [Henshaw, 1998]. About half of the women who unintentionally became pregnant had been using a regular method of contraception. Emergency contraception can prevent pregnancy if taken within 72 hours of unprotected sex. We can explore the consequences of a decision whether or not to use emergency contraception using decision analysis. If emergency contraception is used, the probability of pregnancy is reduced (but not eliminated). If pregnancy does occur, a predictable proportion of women will chose to terminate the pregnancy.

Some women who continue their pregnancies will miscarry. For the sake of simplicity, we shall ignore the effects of nausea following the use of emergency contraception, and complications such as ectopic pregnancies.

3.1.2 Identify and Bound the Problem

The first step in a decision analysis is to identify the alternative courses of action. In the example we are using, the decision is whether or not to use emergency contraception following unprotected sex. The consequences of this decision that interest us are the numbers of unwanted pregnancies, or more specifically the number of pregnancy terminations and live births that would be avoided through use of emergency contraception. The endpoints of the analysis, therefore, are pregnancy terminations and live births. The time horizon will be limited to an episode of unprotected sex and its unintended consequences, i.e., nine months. The perspective is that of society.

3.1.3 Construct a Decision Tree

Step 2, construction of a decision tree, makes the description of the problem and its elements explicit. The tree begins with the decision node and branches representing the alternative courses of action. Here, the decision is to use or not to use emergency contraception following unprotected sex (Figure 5). Following the use (or not) of emergency contraception, pregnancy may or may not occur. A chance node reflecting these

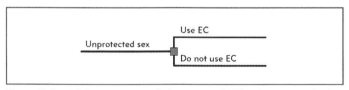

Figure 5. Partial decision tree with decision node. The decision is whether or not to use emergency contraception following unprotected sex.

EC = emergency contraception

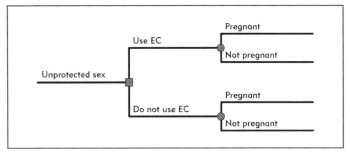

Figure 6. Partial decision tree with chance nodes. Chance nodes reflect the likelihood of pregnancy following unprotected sex.

alternative outcomes is added to each branch emanating from the decision node (Figure 6).

If pregnancy occurs, some women opt for termination and others to continue their pregnancy to term. While for an individual woman this is a decision that must be made, from the per-

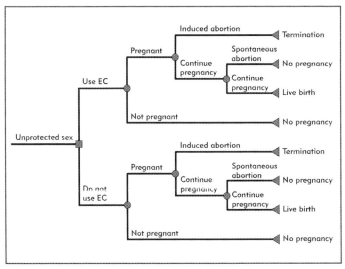

Figure 7. Complete decision tree for the decision of whether to use emergency contraception following unprotected sex.

spective of an observer of a population of women, a measurable proportion of women will chose one option over the other. This proportion might vary according to the composition of the population of women and other factors. The node branching to either pregnancy termination or continuation is thus a chance node.

A certain proportion of women continuing their pregnancies undergo spontaneous abortion; this is also reflected in a chance node. The branches now in the model lead to the endpoints that were decided on in Step 1 – pregnancy termination, live birth, and no pregnancy. The last step in creating the decision tree, therefore, is to add the terminal nodes (Figure 7). The decision tree describing the problem we identified and bounded in Step 1 is now complete.

3.1.4 | Collect the Information to Fill the Decision Tree

In the case of the decision tree in Figure 7, the information sought is a probability value for each chance node. The prob-

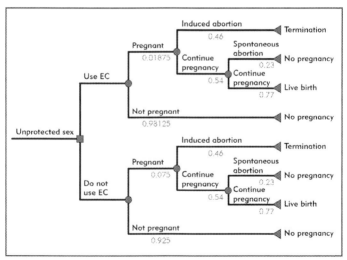

Figure 8. Decision tree (see Figure 7) with probabilities added.

ability estimates are displayed beneath the branches of the decision tree, as seen in Figure 8.

In Figure 8, the probabilities of conception with and without emergency contraception are taken from a clinical trial of emergency contraception versus a control group without emergency contraception. The probabilities of induced and spontaneous abortion are obtained from state statistics [Marciante, 2001]. A more extensive description of information sources is given in Chapter 6.

3.1.5 | Analyze the Decision Tree

We will analyze the tree by calculating the probability of reaching the outcome represented by each of the terminal nodes. This is done by tracing the branches from each terminal node

Decision	Probability				Outcome
	Pregnancy	Induced abortion	Spontaneous abortion		
EC	0.01875	0.46		0.0086	Termination
EC	0.01875	0.54	0.23	0.0023	No pregnancy
EC	0.01875	0.54	0.77	0.0078	Unplanned birth
EC	0.98125			0.9813	No pregnancy
				0.0164	**SUM: unwanted pregnancy***
No EC	0.075	0.46		0.0345	Termination
No EC	0.075	0.54	0.23	0.0093	No pregnancy
No EC	0.075	0.54	0.77	0.0312	Unplanned birth
No EC	0.925			0.9250	No pregnancy
				0.0657	**SUM: unwanted pregnancy***

Table IV. Analysis of decision to use emergency contraception (EC). Analysis of the decision tree shown in Figure 8 (see text).

* Sum of probabilities of pregnancy terminations and unplanned births. The value is 1 minus the sum of probabilities of "no pregnancy"

backwards to the beginning of the tree; the probabilities along these branches are multiplied together to produce the probability of the outcome. These calculations can be performed using a spreadsheet. The spreadsheet has a row for each terminal node and a column for each chance node plus a column for the calculated probability of the outcome.

The spreadsheet corresponding to the decision analysis in Figure 8 is shown in Table IV.

The probability of an induced abortion if emergency contraception is used (corresponding to the top row of Table IV and the uppermost branch line of Figure 8) is 0.01875 x 0.46 = 0.0086 (Note that there are blank cells in the Table where a particular chance node does not occur along the branch line). The outcome for the second and forth rows of Table IV is the same ("No pregnancy") and the probabilities are added together: the probability of no pregnancy if emergency contraception is used is 0.0023 + 0.9813 = 0.9836. Similarly, the probability of "No pregnancy" if emergency contraception is not used is: 0.0093 + 0.9250 = 0.9343. The probability of an unwanted pregnancy (sum of pregnancy terminations and unplanned births) is 0.0164 if emergency contraception is used and 0.0657 if it is not (Table IV).

The consequences, in terms of induced abortions and unplanned births, of the decision to use or not to use emergency contraception for a hypothetical population of 10,000 women are shown in Table V. The use of emergency contraception would prevent 259 induced abortions and 234 unplanned births per l0,000 women who had had unprotected sex.

	Induced abortions	Unplanned births
EC	86	78
No EC	345	312
Difference	-259	-234

Table V. Outcomes of decision to use emergency contraception (EC) per 10,000 women.

Any measurement should be expressed in terms of a point estimate and an indication of its reliability. For instance, in descriptive statistics a mean (point estimate) and range, standard deviation, or 95% confidence interval may be provided. The decision analysis described above has yielded a point estimate of the number of unintended pregnancies prevented by emergency contraception. The reliability of such a point estimate is made difficult to calculate by the (usually) large number of probabilities involved in the model. A point estimate was used for each of the probabilities in the model, but of course there is a range of likely values for each of the probabilities.

Sensitivity analysis determines the effect on the result of varying the probability estimates through the range of their possible or likely values. In a one-way sensitivity analysis, the probabilities at each chance node in the decision tree are varied across their range of values one at a time. This process determines the sensitivity of the results to changes in the assumptions in the model and can identify the most critical assumptions in the

Example

In our decision analysis of the use of emergency contraception, the point estimate of the probability of spontaneous abortion was 0.23. The range of values for this probability is 0.17-0.29 [Marciante, 2001]. Inspection of the decision tree shows that changing the probability of spontaneous abortion does not affect the number of induced abortions but does affect the number of live births. Substituting first the upper limit estimate (0.29) and then the lower limit estimate (0.17) for the value 0.23 used in the initial calculation, we find that the difference in the number of unplanned births (without emergency contraception minus with emergency contraception) varies between 216 and 252 (the point estimate was 234). The spontaneous abortion rate, thus, does not critically affect the reduction in the number of unplanned births attributable to the use of emergency contraception.

model, i.e., those that have the greatest effect on the results. The following is an example of one-way sensitivity analysis. Two-way and three-way and other forms of sensitivity analysis are discussed below. Sensitivity analysis will be further described in Chapter 6.

▓▓▓ Influence Diagrams

It is sometimes useful to draw an influence diagram before constructing a detailed decision tree. An influence diagram makes specific the decision to be taken, the outcome of interest, and the chance elements that influence the outcome. Figure 9 shows an influence diagram corresponding to the decision tree in Figure 8. The only outcome of interest in Figure 9 is live births following unprotected sex (induced abortion was also an endpoint in the decision analysis shown in Figure 9). The outcome is affected by the chance occurrences of pregnancy, induced abortion, and spontaneous abortion. The decision, chance elements, and outcome are presented as a square, circles, and a lozenge shape, respectively.

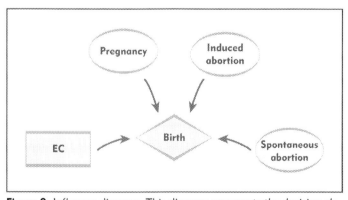

Figure 9. Influence diagram. This diagram represents the decision element and chance elements influencing the outcome of unwanted birth.
EC = emergency contraception

▓▓▓ Markov Models

The decision analysis shown in Figure 8 represents a single, linear chain of events transpiring over a single time period. Some diseases, however, progress gradually over a period of years, while the risk of the outcome of interest, for instance, coronary death, increases with age. Markov analysis is appropriate for such problems.

Markov analyses use tree diagrams similar to those used in simple decision analysis. However, the elements of the problem are first mapped out in a Markov diagram similar to an influence diagram. Figure 10 shows a Markov diagram representing the progression of congestive heart failure. The Markov model consists of states (ovals) and transitions (arrows).

In Figure 10, there are four states: well, early stage heart failure, late stage heart failure, and dead from heart failure, where

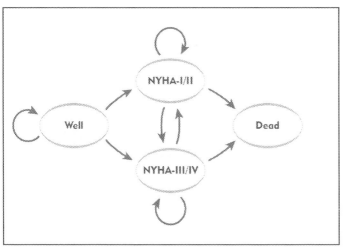

Figure 10. Markov transition state diagram for patients with heart failure. Markov diagram based on study by van Hout et al. [van Hout, 1993]. For simplicity, NYHA classes I and II have been combined, as have NYHA classes III and IV.

NYHA = New York Heart Association class for heart failure

early and late stage heart failure are represented by New York Heart Association (NYHA) class I/II and III/IV, respectively. Time is broken down into a series of sequential periods or cycles; within each cycle, an individual must be in one of the four states; transitions between the states occur at the end of each cycle. Individuals in the "well" state can transit into either of the NYHA class states or remain in the well state (represented by an arrow exiting from and circling back into the well state). Similarly, individuals in the NYHA-I/II state can remain in that state, progress into the NYHA-III/IV state, or enter the "dead" state at the end of each cycle. Needless to say, individuals cannot exit the dead state. Probabilities must be assigned for each transition. Since time is modelled as a series of cycles of equal length, the probabilities can be different at each cycle, so that they can be made dependent on the age of individuals entering the model. Markov models in which probabilities are time dependent are called Markov process models.

3.3.1 Example: Economic Evaluation of Cinacalcet in the Treatment of Secondary Hyperparathyroidism

An illustrative example of the application in pharmacoeconomics of a probabilistic, patient-level model based on Markov cycles is the economic evaluation of cinacalcet in the treatment of secondary hyperparathyroidism (SHTP) for chronic kidney patients in the Italian context [Eandi, 2010]. In dialysis patients considered in the study, the standard treatment, consisting of D vitamin sterols and phosphate binders, is compared with a new treatment where cinacalcet is included. This drug acts as a regulator of levels of plasma PTH, and indirectly of serum calcium (Ca) and phosphorus (P), by controlling the parathyroid activity, thus being associated with clinical benefit, in terms of cardiovascular (CV) and fracture protection. However, the cinacalcet regimen is more expensive than standard care and this creates the necessity for a comprehensive pharmacoeconomic evaluation of its possible adoption. For this purpose, the

48

novel probabilistic model proposed by Eandi et al. [Eandi, 2010] simulates the effect of cinacalcet on the variation of PTH, Ca and P levels on individual patients, and correlates these levels with main clinical endpoints like mortality and morbidity resting upon published evidence.

The model consists of a decision tree scheme (designed with the TreeAge 2009 software) with two independent arms representing the standard and the cinacalcet treatment course in Markov cycles: SHTP, SHTP with parathyroidectomy and death represent the available states of the Markov chain where the main clinical events (CV event, fracture, parathyroidectomy) may be experienced. The simulation spans over a time horizon equal to the whole patients' lifetime, divided in 8-weeks cycles. The outcomes chosen to measure the effectiveness of the cinacalcet and standard treatment are the average time below the recommended KDOQI range (TiR), of PTH, Ca, P, Ca x P [Eknoyan, 2003]: PTH ≤ 300 pg/ml, Ca < 9.5 mg/dl, P < 5.5 mg/dl, and Ca x P lower than 55 $(mg/dl)^2$.

At each iteration one patient is created with his/her unique initial baseline attributes (gender, initial age, PTH, Ca, P level) and sent to both the standard and cinacalcet arm, so that the simulation runs on the very same cohort. During the iteration, patients parameters may change in time thereby affecting probabilities and events rates; the short term variation (weeks) of PTH, Ca, P level of generated individuals with respect to the baseline values are assigned sampling the results of the European multicenter, randomized, open-label OPTIMA study [Messa, 2008] conducted on hemodialysis patients. The model then associates parameter concentrations to relative risk (RR) of events (e.g. mortality), also considering the dependence of subsequent events on prior event occurrence (in CV hospitalization or fracture) and the correlations between different events (the effect of parathyroidectomy on mortality and fracture rate). Mortality and morbidity rates are constantly updated by updating RR factors, in turn adjusted on current PTH and mineral levels, probabilistically sampled for each simulated patient on distributions and data extracted from literature. Internal and

Measure of effectiveness (TiR), utility (LE, QALE) and cost (€)	Cinacalcet group Mean (SD)	Standard group Mean (SD)	Differences Mean (SD)
TiR PTH < 300 pg/ml	5.45 (6.61)	0.19 (0.80)	5.26 (6.59)
TiR Ca < 9.5 mg/dl	6.89 (6.81)	3.26 (5.49)	3.63 (6.87)
TiR P < 5.5 mg/dl	5.86 (6.80)	4.16 (5.93)	1.70 (6.66)
TiR Ca x P < 55 (mg/dl)^2	6.96 (6.87)	4.60 (6.12)	2.36 (6.58)
TiR All	2.72 (5.57)	0.04 (0.34)	2.68 (5.55)
LE (LYs)	9.15 (6.33)	7.95 (5.9)	1.20 (3.75)
QALE (QALYs)	5.84 (5.04)	4.95 (4.54)	0.89 (2.59)
Costs (€) w/o dialysis	51,756 (52,481)	23,595 (25,142)	29,161 (47,277)
Costs (€) with dialysis	294,273 (210,108)	234,273 (177,400)	60,000 (127,831)

Table VI. Effectiveness, utility outcomes and final discounted costs with 10,000 iterations, in terms of time in recommended KDOQI range.

	ICER (cost w/o dialysis)	ICER (cost with dialysis)
TiR PTH (pts-y)	5,354	11,407
TiR Ca (pts-y)	7,754	16,520
TiR P (pts-y)	16,556	35,275
TiR Ca x P (pts-y)	11,947	25,454
TiR all (pts-y)	10,525	22,425
LE (LY)	23,473	50,012
QALE (QALY)	31,616	67,361

Table VII. ICER values calculated for 10,000 iterations according to the various possible definitions of effectiveness and utility: values expressed in Euro versus discounted patient-years (for TiR), life years (for LE), or Quality Adjusted Life Years (for QALE).

50

external validation of the model performed with data from literature confirms the reliability of the model.

Costs and outcomes predicted by the model, discounted at a 3.5% annual rate (Table VI) are obtained as summary statistics of 10,000 iterations.

The benefit of the health treatment is estimated also in term of utility: predicted life expectancy (LE) is weighted by the utility values of end stage renal disease and dialysis (Table VI) obtained from published literature.

Finally, in order to decide the possible adoption of the cinacalcet based treatment, the incremental cost-effectiveness ratio (ICER) has been calculated (Table VII). When considering LE, the average ICER of cinacalcet vs. standard treatment resulted 23,473€/LY, while if considering QALE the average ICER was 31,616€/QALY (Table VI).

3.4 Discrete-event Simulation

In discrete-event simulation (DES), the operation of a system is represented as a chronological sequence of events. Each event occurs at an instant in time and marks a change of state in the system [Robinson, 2004].

DES was originally developed in the 1960s in the fields of industrial engineering while applications in health care have increased over the last 40 years [Jacobson, 2006] (applications relating to biologic models and physiology, process redesign and optimization, geographic allocation of resources, trial design, policy evaluation, and survival modelling, and also in health technology assessments). Key points in discrete-event simulation are entities, events and time:

  ※ **entities** are the objects that can experience the events defining the model structure (typically patients);

  ※ **events** are defined as things that can happen to an entity during the simulation. Events can be, for example, adverse drug reaction, occurrence of clinical conditions (e.g., a stroke) or progression of a disease to a new stage. Markov states can also be considered as events;

* **time** does not flow continuously but is fixed when an event occurs. Events duration is simulated using probabilistic distributions fitted to set of real data (if available) or to mean $\pm$ SD.

3.4.1 | Example of a DES Model in Pharmacoeconomics: Cost-effectiveness of Glutamine Dipeptide for Critically III Patients

The analysis of effectiveness and cost-effectiveness of supplemental glutamine dipeptide in total parenteral nutrition (TPN) therapy for critically ill patients performed by Pradelli et al. [Pradelli, 2012b] is a representative case of a pharmacoeconomics study where a DES model is developed. Several works (cited in [Pradelli, 2012b]) show that alanyl-glutamine (Ala-Gln) in TPN therapy of critically ill patients reduce mortality, infection rate and shorten intensive care unit (ICU) and hospital lengths of stay (LOSs) as compared to standard TPN regimens. The main aim of the simulation study was to investigate whether the Ala-Gln treatment cost is completely offset by the reduction of hospital and medical costs due to improvements in clinical outcomes. This evaluation is performed within a DES scheme with a patient level approach. In this approach every generated individual concurrently follows the clinical course of standard and supplemented Ala-Gln TPN treatment experiencing common events in each simulation step. The two simulated therapeutic arms differ only quantitatively for the probabilities characterizing events occurrence and duration. Every patients starts in ICU where he/she may, or may not, develop a new nosocomial infection. In either case, the patient admitted to the ICU faces three alternative possibilities: death in the ICU, or recovery and transfer to general ward, or recovery and discharge home. For those transferred to general ward, there are two possibilities left: recovery and discharge, or death. Death and discharge represent the end of patient treatment. The time spent in each

52

treatment arm is not discretized in cycles with fixed time intervals valid for the whole patients cohort (as in case of Markov cycles), but is handled as a time-to-event, specifically sampled for every patient from Weibull distributions fitted to "Progetto Margherita" data, yielding a satisfying goodness-of-fit [GIVITI, 2009].

Patient pathways are shown in Figure 11: time spent in each state depends on the outcome of the state itself, i.e. patients who die in ICU will spend less time in ICU than those who are discharged alive; mathematically, length of stay (LOS) in ICU will be sampled from two different distributions.

All the input values of characteristics and probabilities for every generated patient were randomly sampled (Monte Carlo method) from mathematical distributions fitting data concerning critically ill patients obtained from published works: the baseline outcome rates are extracted from 2007 edition of "Progetto Margherita" [GIVITI, 2007] that reports data regarding more than 60,000 inpatients of 200 Italian ICUs, while the efficacy of supplementation of Ala-Gln in the standard treatment are extracted from a systematically reviewed Bayesian meta-analysis of clinical trials [Pradelli, 2012b].

The costs items yielding the overall treatments cost were calculated from the perspective of Italian hospital and were determined using various data sources actualized to the 2008 values according to the inflation index of ISTAT (the Italian National Institute of Statistics). The cost of Ala-Gln was calculated for every simulated patient on the basis of his/her body weight assuming a dose of 0.5 g/kg/day using the maximum price to Italian hospitals (2,107€/g). Bodyweight and TPN duration were sampled from the population data reported in the trials. Average daily cost to hospital of Italian ICUs (including variable, fixed ICU ward costs and ancillary costs) results equal to €1,289 [Cavallo, 2001] while the average cost in Italian hospital ward is calculated as €707.64 [ASSR, 2003]. As for the cost of infections, only the extra anti-infective treatments cost, i.e. ICU-emerged blood stream infections [Orsi, 2002], is calculated (€1,034.6) because the reduction of cost infection in ICU due to the use of Ala-Gln is already counted for in the consequent reduction of LOS with respect to the standard TPN regimen.

In Table VIII the main clinical outcomes and the costs resulting from the Monte Carlo model simulation conducted for 10,000 patients are summarized. On average, Ala-Gln based TPN therapy would prevent more than one-quarter of deaths and infections and reduce the overall mean LOS by 1.1 day, compared with standard TPN. Furthermore, these findings show that the cost of Ala-Gln nutrition is more than offset by the reduction of ICU and antibiotic costs, resulting in a mean net cost saving of €752 per patient. Therefore it could be concluded that addition of Ala-Gln to standard TPN is expected to domi-

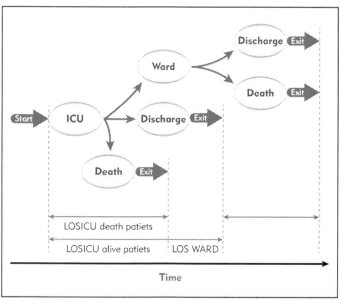

Figure 11. DES diagram based on a cost-effectiveness analysis by Pradelli et al. [Pradelli, 2012b]. Simulated patients enter the model in the ICU and face three alternative outcomes: transfer to a general ward, discharge directly at home or death in the ICU. Those transferred or treated in the general ward are either discharged alive, or die during the hospital stay. The latter two determine the end of patient treatment.

Outcome	Standard TPN Mean (SD)	Standard + Ala-Gln TPN Mean (SD)	Difference Mean (SD)
LOS (days/patients)	25.99 (0.26)	24.91 (0.25)	-1.08 (0.10)
Deaths/10,000 pts	3,446 (208)	2,460 (159)	-986.01 (57.14)
Infections/10,000 pts	1,878 (391)	1,377 (287)	501.41 (106.71)
Overall costs (€/patient)	**24,161 (3,523)**	**23,409 (3,345)**	**-752.08 (307.30)**
ICU	12,925.48 (2,554.33)	11,669.13 (2,308.10)	-1,256.35 (255.08)
Antibiotics	193.73 (56.81)	142.00 (41.62)	-51.72 (15.36)
Supplementation	0 (0)	602.95 (175.79)	602.95 (175.79)
Ward (pre-ICU)	2,905.55 (612.67)	2,905.55 (612.67)	0 (0)
Ward (post-ICU)	8,136.51 (1711.83)	8,089.56 (1,698.92)	-46.95 (65.05)
Overall costs/survivor (€)	**36,905 (5,535)**	**31,061 (4,496)**	**-5,844 (1,162)**

Table VIII. Costs, effectiveness and cost-effectiveness results for Ala-Gln + TPN versus TPN alone in critically ill ICU patients based on model simulation.

nate standard TPN alone, presenting better clinical and economic outcomes. Internal validation of the model performed with observed clinical data strengthen the reliability of the model; the variation of input cost and clinical parameters in one-way sensitivity and in scenario analyses tested the robustness of the results.

3.5 ░ Agent-based Models

In an individual or agent-based (AB) model the status of each individual is explicitly tracked over time. These types of models treat individuals as discrete entities who do not move between compartments but rather change their internal state (e.g., susceptible, infected) based on their interactions. Furthermore, AB models can incorporate population heterogeneity relatively easily, and also have the flexibility to assess complex interventions. Individuals evolving in an AB model are called **agents**. An agent is defined with the following characteristics [Niazi, 2011]:

- **activity**: each agent independently acts following the rules assigned in the simulation and its own pre-programmed behavior. Agents may interact or exchange information with other agents; these interactions may have particular effects on the agent, including its destruction or change in goal-seeking behavior;

- **autonomy**: each agent can make independent decisions in accordance with rules assigned in the simulation;

- **heterogeneity**: generally each agent is created as a member of a limited set of common templates, but it develops individuality through interactions.

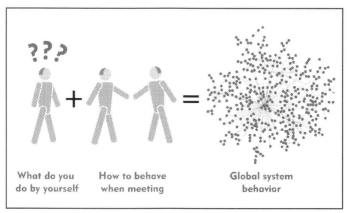

Figure 12. Illustrative representation of an AB model: rules of conduct of a single agent when alone and when interacting with other agents that are assigned *a priori* (but may change due to interaction or learning). Then the global behavior of the whole population (framed network with dots corresponding to agents) naturally arises without external constraints.

Stage for agents behaviors is called **environment**. Environment may change dynamically according to the actions of the agents but these changes occur passively, rather than in the active fashion of agent evolution in time. The state of the environment evolves dynamically, but only in response to the actions of the agents; in sum, agents are active while the environment is passive.

Agent-based modeling allows to incorporate and evaluate complex behaviors and interactions, and as such permits to effectively model complex phenomena [Miller, 2007]. Global system evolution is not modeled *a priori* but it depends on a "few" rules that are assigned to each agent (Figure 12).

BUDGET IMPACT ANALYSIS

Lorenzo Pradelli
AdRes Health Economics and Outcomes Research, Torino, Italy

4.1 Introduction

While CEA and CUA indicate the way to effectively allocate the available resources evaluating the efficiency of a technology, they do not respond to the question whether the new health care intervention is financially viable. In order to help the decision maker to assess if the efficient new health technology may be affordable, it is necessary to estimate the financial consequences within a specific context.

Budget impact analysis (BIA) predicts how a change in the mix of interventions used to treat a particular health condition will impact the trajectory of spending on that condition. In the last years BIA's demand increased, because decision makers must deal with poor financial resources, and BIA is helpful to assess if the new health care intervention may reduce resources utilization in the short term.

«The purpose of BIA is to provide valid computing frameworks that allow users to understand the relation between the characteristics of their setting and the possible budget consequences of a new health technology or a change in usage of current health technologies» [Mauskopf, 2007].

BIA's aims are:

* estimating the financial consequences of a health care intervention;

* understanding the relation between the characteristics of a health scenario and the possible consequences on budget;

BIA's applications comprise, but are not limited to, the following:

- comparing either a new health care intervention with current treatments or change in usage of current health technology;
- estimating the financial consequences of a guideline in a particular health care scenario with the goal of showing if the clinical approach in adherence to guideline is affordable;
- synthesizing the available knowledge at a particular point in time and providing a specific range of predictions based on realistic estimates of the input parameters.

Thus, BIA results should reflect scenarios that consist of specific assumptions and data inputs of interest to the decision-maker, especially those who are responsible for national, regional, or local health care budgets.

The modeling of a BIA can be illustrated in steps:

- Measure the total population at start where the BIA must assess the outcomes: it may be one country, region or local area.
- Estimate the sick population (incidence and/or prevalence) in that area.
- Select the target population, i.e. patients eligible to receive the treatment whose budget impact is to be estimated.
- Analyze the amount of resources used in the current scenario and assess the amount of resources used with the treatment of interest.
- Apply these costs to obtain the overall cost for each scenario: the difference between two arms of interest is the budget impact estimate.

Aspects as efficacy and safety might originate from clinical trials or better from meta-analyses, but other inputs, such as incidence and/or prevalence of disease, rescue medication use, hospitalized patients, conditions for reimbursing that change country by country or even region by region are local and derive from epidemiological sources or cross-sectional studies or market research.

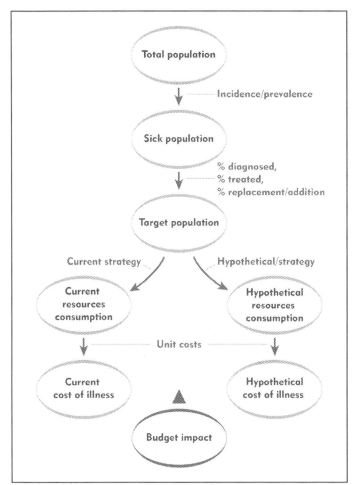

Figure 13. BIA steps. Modified from [Mauskopf, 2007].

A good budget impact model (BIM) must be flexible: it should allow comparing scenarios in which new interventions are added or substituted to either all existing interventions or only those in a particular drug class, in various proportions (different treatment mix scenarios); it should be designed to allow for examination of the effect of alternative assumptions about the nature and size of the treated population, which may also be allowed to evolve (dynamic cohort – patient enter or leave the model whether they preserve or not the inclusion criteria); it should allow for subgroup analysis by incorporating aspects such as disease severity, comorbidities, age, gender, etc.; and it must permit to estimate the budget impact after varying time spans from the intervention introduction (often considering the expected adoption curve, i.e. the evolution of market shares over time).

4.2 Example: Budget Impact Analysis of Clinical Guidelines in COPD Patients

The Global Initiative for Chronic Obstructive Lung Disease (GOLD) guidelines are in general well accepted by the Italian scientific community; however some contradictory data seem to show that in the actual clinical practice they are far from being widely applied yet. This awareness induces the arising of a complex question to be answered: how could be the economic impact related to the full scale application of GOLD guidelines?

Objective of the presented study was to answer this question by simulating perfect adherence to GOLD guidelines by means of a Budget Impact Model [Zaniolo, 2010].

Following the flow of (Figure 13):

- **Total population** is the population over 45 years of age resident in the year 2009 on the Italian territory (27,808,857 citizens).

- **Sick population** is constituted by all Italian COPD patients aged 45 or more (1,262,113 patients). The numerousness of the cohort is calculated from COPD prevalence data, stratified by age and sex in Italy according to the 2009 Health Search Report. The cohort was closed: incident patients are not considered in the model.

※ **Target population** corresponds to the entire sick population (uncommon case). This population enters into a Markov chain model and transits between five states reproducing the GOLD classification of COPD severity plus an absorbing death state and is followed over a 3-year time horizon. The cohort is dynamic: progression probabilities between GOLD states (only from lower to higher severity) are incorporated, as is the mortality rate of the cohort (based on the natural mortality table of the Italian population, factored by specific relative risk values in function of the GOLD state).

※ The model simulates that the same target population is managed under **current** or **hypothetical strategies**. The current strategy is defined in order to reproduce the actual pattern of health care resource consumption and related costs for the COPD management. The hypothetical strategy, defined GL adherence strategy, reproduces the main variations required to improve the adoption of the guidelines in the real clinical practice.

※ **Current resources consumption** is estimated based on:

· the frequency of spirometry-based diagnosis data, provided by three Italian local health units; over a total of 1,725 patients, 61% is staged by spirometry, 26% by clinical classification, and 13% is not staged;

· the real practice drug consumption data, provided by the same local health units, in terms of DDD per patient/year for each therapeutic class and for GOLD stage;

· frequency of required visits to both general practitioners and specialist, emergency unit accesses, ordinary hospital admissions and Day Hospital services, also detailed by GOLD stage. The consumption of these resources is taken from an Italian observational study, considering the 12 months preceding patients monitoring by specialist centers.

* **GL adherence strategy resources consumption** is expected to be driven by:
  - the use of spirometry test to diagnose and stage all patients;
  - the switch of the entire cohort to a well organized patient management plan, either done by the family practitioner or by a specialist. In Italy there are no official standards on COPD management; the model assumes that this management plan could correspond to an initial pneumologist visit, during which relevant clinical data are collected, and the disease management is revised in terms of follow-up schedule (yearly spirometry testing), life style advice, and drug therapy;
  - the aim to estimate the revision of the prescribed drug regimen; considering that guideline recommendations are somewhat generic, authors have used information from an expert Delphi panel, that estimated the mean theoretical requirement of ATC R03 subclasses for each patients according to the severity stage.

The change in other health care resources (visits, hospital admissions) consumption, induced by the improved therapeutic appropriateness, was modeled according to the already cited observational study.

Unit costs are calculated from the perspective of the third party payer. Drug costs have been calculated by applying market share-weighed DDD cost per R03 subgroup to the estimated consumptions. Other health services are valued according to local current tariffs. The in-depth re-evaluation of the patient is monetized based on an Italian prospective micro-costing study (€85.40), in order to differentiate it from the cost of a routine visit (€20.87).

In the GL adherence scenario, the initial clinical evaluation induces an emerging cost not included in the current practice. A further cost increase, compared to current strategy, is related

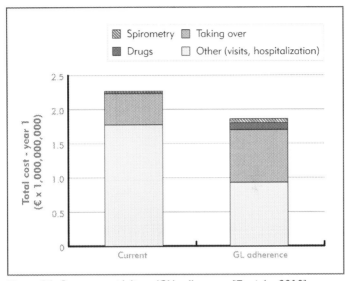

Figure 14. Costs vs. guidelines (GL) adherence [Zaniolo, 2010].

to an improved diffusion of spirometry-based diagnosis and to an expected increase in LABA/ICS combinations consumption. The resulting **hypothetical cost of illness** is equal to 1,863 million Euros. On the other side, the current strategy presents a largely greater expense related to a higher frequency of visits and hospitalizations (+20-54% compared to hypothetical strategy), enough to show a **cost of illness** of 2,273 million Euros. The difference between the current and the hypothetical total cost represents the **budget impact**. As shown in Figure 14, for the first year the model estimates a net balance in favor of GL adherence strategy of about 410 million Euros (some 18% of the current cost). Subsequently this figure slightly decreases, with an estimated saving of 364 and 323 million Euros in the second and third year, respectively.

5 PATIENT REPORTED OUTCOMES

Anke-Peggy Holtorf
PhD, MBA; Health Outcomes Strategies GmbH, Basel Switzerland

*Measure your health by your sympathy
with morning and spring.*
Henry David Thoreau

5.1 Introduction

Contemporary health care systems in general strive for univer-
sal access to health care combined with a high level of quality and equity while, at the same time, facing the challenge of
dwindling funding (economic scarcity). Increasing numbers of
people (especially with an aging population that is living longer) are utilizing health care services and products, expecting
optimal treatment leading to a high level of health and well-
being and a greater longevity. At the same time, the number
of technologies accessing the health care market and seeking
reimbursement is proliferating. For each of the new technologies, policy makers, payers, and finally prescribers, have to decide on utility and value. As with other investment decisions,
they seek to understand what they get for their money. In other
words, they need to understand the cost-benefit relationship
of the new technology or technologies compared with what is
already available. In addition and at least as important as the
budget-related need to understand the cost impact of the new
technology, is the assessment of the expected impact on the
future health status of the patients. How can we measure that?
The recommendation of Thoreau (to measure health by person-
al sympathy with morning and spring) sounds quite straight for-
ward and rather simplistic, yet the development of a commonly
accepted practice is far more complex. While other Chapters in
this book deal with the economic aspects of the question, this

Chapter will focus on the question of which kind of outcomes measures from the patient's perspective can help to determine the beneficial effect of health care interventions.

5.2 From Biological Measures to Patient Reported Outcome

Historically, decisions about adopting new technologies were mostly based on efficacy measures, which, in many cases, could be surrogate measures for effectiveness. **Efficacious** treatments provide positive results in a controlled experimental research trial. An "efficacious" treatment approach means that a study produced good outcomes, which were identified in advance, in a controlled experimental trial, often in highly constrained conditions. In contrast, **effective** treatments provide positive results in a usual or routine care condition that may or may not be controlled for research purposes but may be controlled in the sense of specific activities are undertaken to increase the likelihood of positive results. Effectiveness studies use real-world clinicians and patients, and patients who have multiple diagnoses or needs.

Today patient-centered decisions have moved into the focus of discussion, implying that criteria used to make decisions should be relevant to patients. While patients are generally less guided by surrogate outcomes such as HbA1c levels or blood pressure, they are usually more interested in questions around "length of life" or "quality of life" including factors like the degree of suffering, or the degree of independence and social functioning they can maintain with their disease.

5.3 Quality of Life, Health Related Quality of Life, and Patient Reported Outcomes

Whereas length of life or mortality are endpoints which can sooner or later be measured using a numerical scale, quality of life in general is a broad-ranging concept that describes the degree of well being impacted by many factors such as environment, family, work, social status, or health status as depicted in Figure 15. Within the field of health care, quality of life is often regarded in terms of how it is negatively affected by an individual's health, whereas the "health" had already been defined in 1948 by WHO as «a state of complete physical, mental, and social well-being, and not merely the absence of disease or infirmity» [World Health Organization, 1948].

HRQoL is a composite measure of the individual's physical health or biologic functioning, emotional or psychological state, level of independence, social relationships, and environmental forces. Medical conditions as well as the treatment of medical conditions are expected to influence the HRQoL [Khanna, 2007].

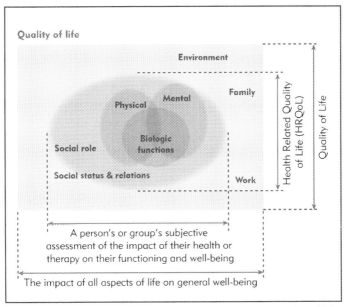

Figure 15. Definition of quality of life and health related quality of life. Adapted from [Khanna, 2007; Patrick, 2007].

For the determination of HRQoL in early QoL research, in general, data were collected via staff-administered surveys. With increasing experience in questionnaire development and validation, direct patient self-reporting became the preferred method. The patient's perspective regarding the effectiveness of a treatment became more important than the assumed objectivity thought to be achieved through a professional interviewer. Some treatment effects are known only to the patient, e.g. localized leg pain, mild swelling, or avoidance behavior. Such aspects of treatment benefit might be lost if the patient's perspective is first interpreted by a health professional. In addition, some changes in clinical endpoints may not always correlate well with the patient's perception of his/her health status. For example, the 6 minute walk test used to determine the functional exercise capacity of patients with moderate-to-severe heart or lung disease may not reflect the patient's subjective ability to perform daily activities [ATS, 2002]. Thus, HRQoL becomes an outcomes measure directly reported by the patient, i.e. a "patient reported outcome measure" (PROM).

According to the US Food and Drug Administration (FDA) a patient reported outcome (PRO) is a type of data measuring any aspect of a patient's health status that comes directly from the patient (i.e. without the interpretation of the patient's responses by a physician or anyone else) [Food and Drug Administration, 2006]. The European Medicines Agency (EMA) similarly defined a PRO as "any outcome directly evaluated by the patient and based on patient's perception of a disease and its treatment(s)" [European Medicines Agency, 2005]. PRO is hence the general reference to the concept (outcome) of interest [Patrick, 2011a].

PROs can be both single and multi-dimensional, whereas HRQoL is determined in multidimensional instruments such as questionnaires or surveys, diaries, or interviews. In addition to HRQoL, patient reported outcomes can be physiological measures, patient satisfaction or other any experiences assessed and reported directly by the patient [Patrick, 2011a; Patrick, 2007]. Data are generated with PRO instruments, which encompass questionnaires in combination with all guidance or documentation on the questionnaire [Patrick, 2011a].

PRO measurement tools evolved from general HRQoL tools to be more disease-specific and symptoms oriented and have a broader range of applications in the clinical practice and decision making. PRO-endpoints are even accepted as a basis for some drug labelling claims. In the USA, the FDA issued a first guidance on PROMs in 2006 (draft) and 2009 (final) to clarify the role of patient-reported data in the drug approval process and to refine standards for PRO instrument development [Food and Drug Administration, 2006; Food and Drug Administration, 2009; Trotti, 2007]. The EMA issued a Regulatory Guidance for the "Use of Health Related Quality Of Life (HRQOL) Measures in the Evaluation of Medicinal Products" in 2005 [European Medicines Agency, 2005].

Last not least, PROMs are relevant to patients and help them to understand the impact of their disease and of its treatment in comparison to treatment alternatives. For example «What will happen to the pain when I take this medication? Which side effects do I have to expect? How tired will I be? Can I live longer – or longer at home – when I take this medication? What does it mean to my family, to my work, or my social network?».

5.4   PRO Dimensions

In 1995, Wilson and Cleary conceptualized a model of patient-related outcomes by defining five levels of health outcomes with increasing complexity [Wilson, 1995; Poolman, 2009]:

  * biological and physiological variables;
  * symptom status;
  * functional status;
  * general health perceptions; and
  * overall quality of life.

Each increasingly higher level can be modulated by individual characteristics (individual symptom experiences, motivation, values and preferences) and by environmental characteristics (social, economic, and psychological support). The traditional health care system focuses on measuring and treating the biological and physiological components while the symptoms are usually the reason why the patient appears in the medical practice. However, patients can have abnormalities on the physiological level, such as osteoporosis, without having symptoms. On the other hand, symptoms may not always correlate with physiological diagnostic findings as can be seen in some cases of chronic pain. Functional status may again not be fully explained by the knowledge of biological factors and symptoms, because of individual and environmental factors; let alone general health perceptions and overall quality of life, which encompass much more than just a reaction to a single health defect. Thus, in outcomes studies, each level of outcomes needs to be addressed with the appropriate measures. Physician-driven diagnostic tests help to describe biological or physiological status or outcomes and, to some degree, the measurement or description of symptoms. Moving towards the more complex levels of outcomes, the measurement will increasingly rely on the patients themselves. Functional status can be measured by using functional tests, but the findings may not be consistent with the patient's perception of his or her functional status. General health perceptions at latest, although often connected to the biological or physiological factors, become fully dependent on the individual self-assessment due to the growing impact of the individual and environmental modulators [Wilson, 1995].

5.5 Every Patient has Individual Health Perceptions

We should however not forget that people's assessment and reporting of their health, and especially of HRQoL, are relative and can be impacted by many different factors such as age, geography, cultural background, income level, gender, family status. This can for instance, be seen in the OECD regular health indicator reports [OECD, 2011]. Figure 16 shows that about two-thirds of the adult respondents of the health status surveys in Mexico and Germany in 2009 rated their health as good or better. In similar surveys in the Slovak Republic, Japan, Portugal and Korea less than half of the adult population rated their health as good or very good. Further differences were seen within the countries:

* men are more likely than women to report a better health except in Australia, New Zealand and Finland;

* positive rating of the own health tends to decrease with age with specific declines after the age of 45 and 65;

* people who are unemployed, retired or inactive report poor or very poor health more often;

* lower level of education and lower level of income usually lead to lower rating of health [OECD, 2011].

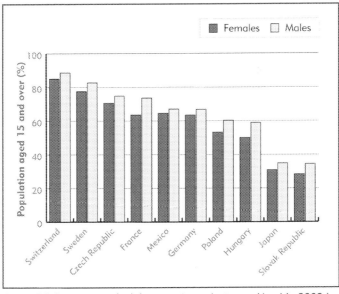

Figure 16. Percentage of adults reporting to be in good health, 2009 (or nearest year) [OECD, 2011].

5.6 Applications of PRO Instruments

HRQoL instruments are used for many different applications, often in chronic (high long-term burden) but also in acute diseases. PROs can:

* Help to acquire extended knowledge on burden of diseases to the patients or their direct or indirect social environment.

* Be used as endpoint in clinical trials (see FDA [Food and Drug Administration, 2006; Food and Drug Administration, 2009] and EMA [European Medicines Agency, 2005; Poolman, 2009] guidances).

* Help to differentiate drug treatments:
  * in terms of marginal differences in drug efficacy or survival rates; or
  * when the competitor drug is more efficacious but may have greater morbidity due to side effects.

* Be used in clinical practice:
  * to monitor outcomes in clinical practice;
  * to support patient-centered decision making in clinical practice;
  * as quality control criteria. For example, in 2009, the UK Department of Health has issued guidance on routinely using PROMs in clinical practice to support providers and primary care commissioners to implement the requirement to collect PROMs contained in the standard NHS contract for acute services [Department of Health, 2009].

* Be used as a criterion in Health Technology Assessment (the use of PROs among 9 key HTA agencies across the globe (PBAC, CADTH, HAS, IQWiG, SMC, NHS Scotland, NICE, DERP, AHRQ) increased steadily, from 11.1% in 2005 to 42.5% in 2011 [Rubinstein, 2012]).

* Support decisions in public policy (via using quality adjusted life years) as used in the UK, Australia, Sweden, or Canada.

* Serve for more direct adverse event reporting. While the patients experience the symptoms of adverse events, they are, in most of the current systems, usually first interpreted by the clinician and intermediate administrative personnel before they are reported in the clinical research database or the pharmacovigilance system. This will shift to a model in which patient-reporting is an important mechanism for monitoring subjective adverse events leading to a potentially higher quality and completeness of collected data while at the same time increasing efficiency of the reporting [Trotti, 2007]. The new pharmacovigilance legislation of the European Union effective from July 2012 requires from all member states to set up systems for direct patient reporting of adverse events [European Medicines Agency, 2012; European Medicines Agency, 2011].

5.7 Identifying an Appropriate Instrument for Measuring PRO

Selecting an outcome instrument starts with the proposed research question and identification of relevant endpoints ("context of use") [Rothman, 2007; Poolman, 2009]. The selection of the instruments most suitable to evaluate the intervention under investigation and the patient population to be included needs to be driven by the research question. In addition, a range of quality criteria as depicted in Table IX can serve as guidance in the selection of an appropriate instrument. For example, Terwee et al. proposed a checklist of quality criteria to evaluate the methodological soundness of patient-reported outcome instruments [Terwee, 2007].

The adequacy of a HRQOL instrument depends on its ability to measure concepts that are relevant to the medical condition, including the important positive and negative concerns of patients undergoing therapy. HRQOL end points, like all other end points, must be indicators of clear and interpretable treatment benefit or harm in clinical trials. There may be situations where no appropriate instrument is available. In this case the development of a new dedicated instrument may be considered but should follow a strict methodological framework. Such frameworks exist in the form of checklists and guidance documents [Patrick, 2011b; Jackowski, 2003; Farnik, 2012; Terwee, 2007; Poolman, 2009].

Table IX summarizes in 5 steps how to develop, apply and report new PRO instruments. The detailed processes have been methodologically described by a Task Force of the International Society of Pharmacoeconomics and Outcomes Research and others, and should be consulted when constructing new instruments [Patrick, 2011b; Rothman, 2007; Jackowski, 2003; Farnik, 2012].

Content/face validity	Do the items in the instrument comprehensively test the research question?
Internal consistency	How much correlation or overlap or redundancy exist between the items of the instrument?
Criterion validity	Do the scores correlate with similar measures in a way that is consistent with the concept hypothesis?
Construct validity	Do the scores correlate with similar measures in a way that is consistent with the concept hypothesis?
Reproducibility	Will repeated measurements (test-retest) in steady populations provide similar answers?
Inter-rater reliability	Will two or more raters obtain the same results with the same instrument?
Intra-rater reliability	Will the same rater obtain the same results when using the instrument at different occasions?
Responsiveness	Will the instrument detect important changes over time?
Floor and ceiling effects	How many patients reach the highest or lowest score (so that no change can be detected over time)?
Interpretability	Can qualitative meanings be assigned to quantitative scores?

Table IX. Quality criteria for the selection of patient reported outcome instruments. Adapted from [Terwee, 2007; Patrick, 2011b; Farnik, 2012].

1. Determine context of use	• Disease state • Target population • Context relevant endpoints • Cultural/language or other issues • Framework/scope
2. Research protocol for qualitative outcomes elicitation and analysis	• Target sample characteristics • Data collection methods/setting/location • Material (interview, training, and documentation) • Testing in pilot
3. Interviews, survey, focus groups	• Ethical approval/IRB • Site recruitment, and training • Quality control measures • Data collection • Result documentation
4. Analysis of the qualitative data	• Apply analysis protocol • Interpret results
5. Documentation of outcomes research and results	• Document all previous steps • Present results • Interpret results • Consider limitations and alternatives

Table X. The five steps to elicit and report concepts for new patient-reported outcome instruments according to the ISPOR PRO Good Research Practices Task Force [Patrick, 2011b].

It should be underlined that the results can only correspond to the context of use (Table X) if the patient understands the question and choice of answer in the same way as the researcher interprets them and if they are relevant to them. Documentation of target population input as well as evaluation of patient understanding through cognitive interviewing are important activities to assure content validity [Patrick, 2011b].

5.8 PRO Instruments

The choice of instruments will have a major impact on the usefulness of quality of life and patient reported outcome studies. Selection should be guided by the purpose of the study, by the domains measured, and the populations and pathologies for which they are designed. In addition, there are practical issues, such as the availability in the correct language, copyrights, and

Type of instrument	Example	Purpose	Advantage	Disadvantage
Generic instrument	Short Form 36 (SF-36) Sickness Impact Profile (SIP) Health Utility Index (HUI) EuroQol (Q-5D)	Designed to be used in any disease population Cover a broad aspect of the construct measured	Applicable in many diseases Comparison across disease states possible	Resolution too low to identify (small) differences in a specific dimension
Disease or condition specific instruments	Adult Asthma Quality of Life Questionnaire (AQLQ) Paediatric Asthma Quality of Life Questionnaire (PAQLQ) Gastro-oesopha-geal Reflux Disease Impact Scale (GIS)	Designed to specific quality of life aspects of a specific patient group with a specific disease	High resolution of specific outcomes of interest to the patients with this disease	Cannot be used for analyses across diseases, priority setting or policy related assessments
Health profile	SF-36 SIP	Informs on a range of health or QoL dimensions	Individual Outcomes Score (IOS) Can be used to track changes over time	Result cannot be aggregated in 1 number Difficult for prioritization or health economic comparisons
Health index	HUI EQ-5D	Summarizes health state of QoL into one score across all dimensions analyzed	Single score (scale 1 to 0) allows easier integration Can be used for calculating e.g., cost utility	General for all dimensions Low informative value for patients or physicians

Table XI. Comparison of different types of PRO instruments.

access to instruments. There are a number of organizations that offer a structured library of instruments to facilitate the selection such as the "Patient Reported Outcomes and Quality of Life Instruments Database (PROQOLID)" [Anonymous, 2012b; Emery, 2005] or the "Patient-Reported Outcomes Measurement Group" [Anonymous, 2012a].

Table XI offers a basic categorization of PRO instruments. The primary distinction is between those that are generic and hence widely applicable, and those that are specific to particular health problems or populations. The instruments or questionnaires can be unidimensional to analyze one specific dimension or construct or multidimensional to analyze several dimensions or constructs. Typical dimensions are: emotional functioning (or disability), physical functioning, social functioning, mobility, mental functioning, or symptoms (impairments) [Fayers, 2007]. Each dimension can be assessed by one or several items (questions). Many questionnaires also ask one or more general health status or quality of life questions (e.g., «How would you rate your health on a scale between 0=death and 100=perfect health?»). A typical structure of a PRO instrument is outlined in Figure 17.

Generic PRO tools typically assess HRQoL or patient perceptions of health care. Examples for such PRO instruments are

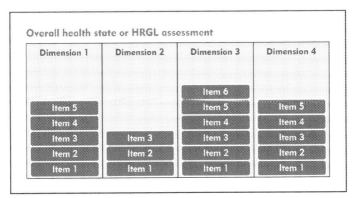

Figure 17. Typical structure of a PRO instrument.

the Short Form 36 (SF-36) Health Survey [Ware, 1992], the
Sickness Impact Profile (SIP) [Bergner, 1981], the Nottingham
Health Profile [Hunt, 1980], the Health Utilities Index [Furlong,
2001] (HUI), the EuroQol (EQ-5D) [Brooks, 1996], and the
Consumer Assessment of Healthcare Providers and Systems
[Squires, 2012] (CAHPS) survey instruments.

Examples of disease specific questionnaire are the Adult Asthma Quality of Life Questionnaire (AQLQ) [Gupchup, 1997],
the Paediatric Asthma Quality of Life Questionnaire (PAQLQ)
[Reichenberg, 2000], or the Gastro-oesophageal Reflux Disease
Impact Scale (GIS) [Jones, 2007].

5.9   When are the Results of PROs Relevant?

Finally, after discussing the principles of PRO instruments for
informing the researcher on health status, health related quality of life, and health care perceptions from the direct patient
perspective, it is important to define when the detected differences are relevant and meaningful. The concept of a "minimal
important difference" (MID) has been developed to support users in defining the lower detection limits for PRO instruments.
MIDs should help to define the smallest difference in score on a
HRQoL instrument that patients perceive as beneficial and that
would mandate, in the absence of troublesome side effects and
excessive cost, a change in the patient's management. Equally,
if the demonstrated difference remains smaller than the MID, it
remains not meaningful even if it is statistically significant [King,
2011]. The MID for a PRO instrument may vary by population
and context, and study applications require the estimation of
different MIDs [Revicki, 2008].

5.10   Summary and Conclusion

In this Chapter, we have given a general overview of patient
reported outcomes. We talked about the need to assess the

value of health intervention from the perspective of the final beneficiary, the patient. We also considered that a health care intervention, which does not make any difference to the patient, may not be a good investment, even if it is less costly than other interventions.

We have looked into the measurement and use of PROs with existing and newly developed instruments and finally looked at different types of instruments. Short overviews like this can only scratch the surface of the wide field of patient-reported outcomes in modern health science, research, and health policy. However, we hope that we have been able to raise some alternative thought about how to measure health and health outcomes. Finally, we may see Thoreau's suggestion on how to measure health as a first hint of a two-dimensional questionnaire with two items asking «How do you like mornings?» and «How do you like spring?» as surrogates for physical, mental, and social implication of many diseases.

6 DATA SOURCES AND ACCOUNTING FOR UNCERTAINTY

Albert Wertheimer
PhD, MBA. Professor of Pharmacy,
Department of Pharmacy Practice, Philadelphia

6.1 Data Sources

In a cost-effectiveness analysis, two kinds of data are needed: probability values for the chance nodes in the decision tree; and an account of the health care resources used and the monetary costs associated with the consequences (branches) stemming from each chance node. Suppose that a health care professional wishes to know the answer to a certain question, such as: is drug X an effective treatment for disease Y in population Z? There are three ways to find an answer: the first is to ask someone; the second is to look the answer up in the literature; and the third is to perform a study designed to find out the answer. All three ways of finding answers are used in pharmacoeconomics. The first method – asking someone who might know – is institutionalized in the form of the augustly named Delphic Panel, which is a panel of experts convened to provide their collective opinion. The Delphic Panel is named after the oracle of Delphi, famed in classical Greece for its cryptic pronouncements that could be interpreted as prophetic only in retrospect. Unless supported by an explicit marshalling of factual data and analysis, mere opinion does not qualify as evidence-based medicine. The second two methods are discussed in this Chapter.

6.1.1 Clinical Epidemiology

Pharmacoeconomic studies usually require data both on costs and effectiveness. The effectiveness data are taken from epidemiological or medical research studies. The design of every medical research study can be classified according to a few fundamental mutually exclusive dichotomies (Table XII).

First, a study may be either observational or experimental. A clinical trial is an experiment – a test of an intervention – in which the investigator interferes with the normal course of events, usually by providing certain people with a treatment they would not otherwise have received. In an observational study, the investigator merely observes events and does not interfere with them. There cannot be, therefore, an "observational trial". Second, the events being studied may have already occurred, in which case the study is a retrospective one, or may not yet have occurred, in which case they will be studied as they happen, i.e., prospectively. An observational study may be either retrospective or prospective but an experimental study can only be prospective – unless, that is, the investigator possesses a time machine in which he visits the past to perform his intervention before returning to the present to collect the results. Third, the observations may refer to a point in time, and are called cross-sectional, or to two or more points in time, and are then called longitudinal. An observational study may be longitudinal or cross-sectional and in both cases may be either prospective or retrospective. An experimental study, however, can only be longitudinal because, however brief in duration it might be, it is an analysis of cause and effect-the "cause" being the intervention being tested, and the "effect" being the clinical outcome being observed which cannot by definition occur at the same point in time. Thus, a clinical trial is a prospective, longitudinal, experimental study.

Investigator involvement	Study design		
	Observational		Experimental
Time perspective	Prospective	Retrospective	Prospective
Time sampling	Longitudinal or cross-sectional	Longitudinal or cross-sectional	Longitudinal

Table XII. Concepts in clinical study design.

The U.S. state and federal governments make available basic demographic information that is often needed in pharmacoeconomic analyses – e.g., the death rate from all causes by age and gender, death rates by cause, etc. The Census Bureau publishes past and projected population demographic data. The National Center for Health Statistics also collects and makes available ongoing national survey data addressing a variety of subjects. These include the National Health Insurance Interview Survey, the National Health and Nutrition Examination Survey, and the National Health Care Surveys.

Much of the information required in a pharmacoeconomic analysis is present in studies published in the medical literature. There are several considerations in extracting data from the literature: determining sources of information, defining a search strategy, categorizing the studies identified, assessing the internal validity of individual reports, assessing the representativeness of the sample of studies identified, and determining the external validity of the data, i.e., whether the data that are valid in the context of the published study are applicable to the setting of the pharmacoeconomic analysis.

Very often, several studies can be identified that yield range of values for the variable of interest. There are two approaches to this situation. First, if there are one or two large, well designed studies (such as randomized controlled trials designed and performed under FDA scrutiny), it is reasonable to consider this as "best evidence" and disregard larger numbers of smaller, statistically underpowered studies or studies with less rigorous designs. Second, the results of several studies can be combined in a meta analysis or systematic review.

Meta-analysis

The term **meta-analysis** is used in a number of different ways but, in essence, it means the statistical pooling of data from several studies. Meta-analysis has its origin in the social sciences. A **systematic review** is a meta-analysis as interpreted by the evidence-based medicine movement. It is performed according to a predefined system or methodology and requires conceptual homogeneity in the design and endpoints of the studies being pooled. One of the most useful sources for meta-analyses of trials of the efficacy of treatments is the Cochrane Database of Systematic Reviews (www.cochrane.org).

What is the difference between a systematic review and a meta-analysis? These methods lie on a continuum, but the use of a standardized "effect size" might be taken as a dividing line between them because it is symptomatic of heterogeneity in the study outcomes. Various effect size statistics have been devised; Hedges' g and Cohen's d are commonly used, in addition

---

Example of systematic review

An example of a systematic review is provided by an investigation of the effects of lipid lowering drugs in the primary prevention of coronary heart disease [Pignone, 2000]. The authors of the review included only long-term randomized controlled trials with, as clinical endpoint, the proportion of the patients who died from coronary heart disease. Three trials of statins were identified, in which about one thousand-to-seven thousand patients were followed for up to about five years. The authors calculated a pooled odds ratio for the effect of statins on coronary heart disease mortality, i.e., the odds of coronary heart disease death while taking statins divided by the odds of coronary heart disease death while taking placebo. This pooled odds ratio was 0.65 with a 95% confidence interval of 0.48 to 0.89, indicating that statins were an effective treatment. This study, published in the *British Medical Journal*, is a good example of a meta-analysis performed under the procedures of a systematic review. The statistical pooling was done with studies that were conceptually homogenous in design, interventions, and endpoints. Purists might object, however, that the studies were heterogeneous in several ways – different statins were administered to different populations during different time periods – and therefore not eligible for statistical pooling. The above is an example of a meta-analysis that is also a systematic review in the tradition of evidence-based medicine. The following is an example of a meta-analysis from the social sciences that diverges from evidence-based medicine in several key ways.

to the Pearson correlation coefficient. The practice of pooling disparate data in meta-analyses as in the above example partly explains why meta-analysis has been seen as controversial. Some authors of systematic reviews eschew statistical pooling of heterogeneous data.

Network meta-analyses or mixed treatment comparison (MTC) enable us to combine trials comparing different sets of treatments, and form a network of evidence within a single analysis [Caldwell, 2005]. The main assumption in network meta-analysis is that relative within-trial treatment effects can be pooled, thus generalizing meta-analysis: instead of solely considering RCTs conducted to investigate the same direct comparison, it infers on the network of available evidence.

The relevance in pharmacoeconomics is related to the possibility to inform simulation modeling about treatment comparisons that have not been (sufficiently) studied in clinical trials.

6.1.3 | Clinical Studies

In extremis, when the required data are not available in the literature, a dedicated study must be performed. Observational studies are often undertaken to determine costs. However, a clinical trial is never undertaken with the sole purpose of determining cost-effectiveness. This is because a cost-effectiveness analysis is only considered **after** effectiveness has first been demonstrated. However, cost data may be collected prospectively in an effectiveness (or efficacy) trial, which is then called a piggyback trial.

6.1.4 | Administrative Databases

Medical information about patients, such as blood pressure, temperature, severity of illness, etc., is usually recorded on paper "charts" and is conveniently accessible only for individual patients or small groups of patients. An alternative is to "follow the money". Every health care transaction that takes place is documented using standard systems of codification, with the ultimate purpose of obtaining payment. This codified information can be used not only to track payments for health care services, but to build a picture of the health care services used by a patient or class of patients, and to infer a picture of the courses of diseases and the effects of the treatments.

The main types of data contained in administrative databases are demographic, diagnostic, procedural, and pharmaceutical. The demographic data is usually limited to the patient's age and gender. The diagnosis the patient receives is entered as a code using the International Classification of Diseases (ICD). The principal diagnosis and a limited number of comorbidities are recorded by their ICD codes. The exact nature of any procedure performed by a physician is documented in terms of a CPT code, and each drug that is prescribed is specified by its National Drug Code (NDC). These data sets also include in-

---

Example: a HMO administrative database analysis

The health care costs of peptic ulcers and bleeding resulting from the prescription of non-steroidal anti inflammatory agents (NSAIDs) for arthritis have been intensively investigated. Johnson et al. estimated the incidence of inpatient and outpatient gastropathies, the services provided to treat them, and the costs of those services for elderly members of a health maintenance organization (HMO) located in the north-west United States [Johnson, 1997]. The data for morbidity and health care resource use were obtained from four automated databases maintained by the HMO: an outpatient pharmacy database, a hospital discharge database, a membership information database, and an outpatient utilization database. These four data sets were linked using the patient identifier tagging each record. The pharmacy and hospital discharge databases contained information for every prescription and inpatient stay, respectively, that occurred. The outpatient database represented a random sample of outpatient encounters abstracted from paper medical records. Costs to the HMO were estimated from the Medicare Cost Report, an aggregate report of costs that includes direct medical and overhead costs related to capital investment, general administration, etc., and which formed the basis for cost based Medicare reimbursements to the HMO. The result of the study was that, for every dollar spent by the HMO on NSAID therapy for the elderly, another 35 cents was spent to treat the adverse gastrointestinal effects of the NSAIDs.

formation on the service provider: the physician's specialty, the setting (primary care, outpatient, inpatient), geographic location, and, if inpatient, patient identifier, a unique number that identifies the recipient of the health care service.

Because of the fragmented nature of the health care system in the United States, however, collating the different data sets into one coherent whole may be problematic for any given population of patients. State Medicaid and Medicare data sets certain comprehensive records for patients covered by this insurance systems, but they only apply to eligible indigent and elderly (65 years and over) patients, respectively. Staff model HMOs also may contain complete data sets. In the case of third-party payment systems, however, the data sets may be dispersed among different payer. Pharmacy data sets may be maintained by Pharmacy Benefit Management companies (PBMs), while numerous health care insurers may maintain hospital and primary care claims data. Collations of private sector health care insurance data sets can be purchased that

---

Example: a private-pay, fee-for-service database analysis

The health care costs associated with the treatment of depression with different classes of antidepressant drug were estimated in a retrospective cohort study [Poret, 2001]. The data source was a proprietary database of medical and pharmacy claims collated from numerous private, fee-for-service health care insurers covering employees of corporate America. Individuals who had a new prescription for an antidepressant drug and a diagnosis of depression within a defined time period (the index period) were identified, and their health care resource use was tracked for the next six months. A diagnosis of depression was indicated by a relevant ICD-9 code in inpatient and outpatient records. Antidepressant drugs were identified by their NDC codes. Costs were compared for antidepressant drug classes using an intent to-treat analysis, i.e., the patient was classified according to the initial antidepressant drug he or she was prescribed in the index period, regardless of whether he or she subsequently switched to another class during the follow-up period.

---

6. Data Sources and Accounting for Uncertainty

offer a complete picture of the encounters of hundreds of thousands of patients with the health care system over defined time periods.

6.1.5 | Financial Data

Administrative data sets contain the dollar (or Euro, etc.) payments made for the health care resources used. These payments are not necessarily the same as the charges made by the payee because of negotiated fee schedules, capitation, etc. List prices of health care goods and services are published by State Medicare systems. In the United States, list prices for drugs are published as average wholesale prices and are also available as retail prices. Data on employee remuneration, which might be needed for an indirect costs analysis, are provided by the Bureau of Labor Statistics.

6.2 Statistical Analysis

Classical statistics is based on hypothesis testing. The hypothesis is made that the observations to be explained are the result purely of chance: this is the null hypothesis. A calculation is then made of the probability that the observations would arise under the null hypothesis and, if that probability is below an arbitrary threshold (most often 1 in 20, or 0.05), the null hypothesis is rejected. The results cannot be explained purely by chance and are said to be "statistically significant".

Note that the above procedure explores the role of random chance and in itself does nothing to assess the role of systematic error (discussed below), which is often more important than random error. Hypothesis testing is not particularly useful in decision analysis, where we need to know the probability of a certain event occurring (such as death from a myocardial infarction) under a certain set of circumstances (such as when a patient has already had one heart attack). The calculation of such conditional probabilities is referred to as **Bayesian analy-**

sis. To the non preconditioned mind, the Bayesian approach may be more intuitive, if less conceptually sophisticated, than hypothesis testing.

6.3 Accounting for Uncertainty

6.3.1 Definition of Error

There are two kinds of error, namely random error and systematic error. Random error is variability in the result caused by random or unpredictable variability in the factors determining the result. Systematic error is a bias in the result caused by nonrandom variability in these factors.

To understand the distinction between the two kinds of error, imagine darts thrown at a dartboard. The random clustering of the darts around the bull's eye (which is the target) represents random error. The tighter the clustering around the bull's eye, the less random error there is. If the darts tend to cluster in the lower right quadrant of the board, for example, there is a systematic error or bias in the thrower's aim.

In this context, the word "error" means variability and does not imply that a preventable mistake has been made. Similarly, the word "bias" does not require a conscious or unconscious human motivation to alter the results.

> **Example**
>
> Several randomly chosen human subjects were given the same dose of a drug. The response of the subjects to the single dose varied greatly and a graph of the drug response versus frequency described a bell curve. Among the factors causing this variability were genetically determined differences among subjects in their ability to absorb, metabolize, and eliminate the drug, and in the interaction of the drug with its tissue target. The subjects varied greatly in their body mass, blood volume, percent body fat, the metabolizing ability of their livers, and in a host of other attributes that modified the action of the drug.

92

6.3.2 | Principal Sources of Error in Clinical Studies

Although many types of bias in the design and conduct of chemical studies have been described, Chalmers has pointed out that most fall into three important categories: selection bias at study entry, selection bias after study entry, and bias in assessing outcomes [Chalmers, 1989] (Table XIII).

6.3.3 | Reducing Error in Clinical Studies

The obscuring of the true result due to random error can be lessened in two ways: by increasing the sample size, and by reducing the variability in the sample. Approaches to reducing systematic error are discussed below.

6.3.4 | Selection Bias in Subjects Entering the Study

Randomization

In a controlled clinical trial, random allocation of subjects to treatments eliminates systematic error at study entry. An imbalance in the allocation of subjects may remain – e.g., more females than males may be assigned to treatment A than to treatment B – simply because of random error, but this may be reduced by increasing the sample size. The process of random allocation is blind to both perceivable and unperceivable differences between subjects, and this is its principal virtue.

Error	Controlled trial	Comparative observational study
Selection bias at study entry	Randomization	Case matching, propensity scoring
Selection bias after study entry	Intent-to-treat analysis	Intent-to-treat analysis, multivariate analysis
Bias in assessing outcomes	Observer blinding, subject blinding	

Table XIII. Means of accounting for systematic error by study design.

Randomization procedure should achieve the following objectives [Lachin, 1988]:

* equal group sizes for adequate statistical power, especially in subgroup analyses;

* low selection bias; the procedure should not allow an investigator to predict how subjects will be assignment in reviewing the previous pairings;

* low probability of confounding (i.e., a low probability of "accidental bias"), which implies a balance in covariates across groups. If the randomization procedure causes an imbalance in covariates related to the outcome across groups, estimates of effect may be biased if not adjusted for the covariates.

No single randomization procedure meets those goals in every circumstance, so researchers must select a procedure for a given study based on its advantages and disadvantages [Roter, 1998]. Randomization procedures are described below.

Simple randomization. Intuitive and commonly used procedure, similar to "repeated fair coin-tossing", also known as "complete" or "unrestricted" randomization. It is robust against both selection and accidental biases. However, its main drawback is the possibility of imbalanced group sizes in small RCTs. It is therefore recommended only for RCTs with over 200 subjects.

Restricted randomization. To balance group sizes in smaller RCTs, some form of restricted randomization is recommended. The major types of restricted randomization used in RCTs are:

* Blocked randomization: the number of subjects in one group versus the other group and the block size are specified; subjects are allocated randomly within each block. For example, a block size of 6 and an allocation ratio of 2:1 would lead to random assignment of 4 subjects to one group and 2 to the other. Unfortunately, even if the block sizes are large and randomly varied, the procedure can lead to selection bias.

* Adaptive biased-coin randomization methods: relatively uncommon methods in which the probability of being

assigned to a group decreases if the group is over-represented and increases if the group is under-represented. The methods are thought to be less affected by selection bias than permuted-block randomization.

Adaptive randomization. Less frequently other two types of adaptive randomization procedures have been used in RCTs:

* Covariate-adaptive randomization: the probability of being assigned to a group varies in order to minimize covariate imbalance. Since only the first subject's group assignment is truly chosen at random, the method does not necessarily eliminate bias on unknown factors.

* Response-adaptive randomization, also known as outcome-adaptive randomization: the probability of being assigned to a group increases if the responses of the prior patients in the group were favorable.

Case Matching

In a comparative observational study, there may be considerable differences between the subjects who received treatment A and those who received treatment B. The investigator can control for perceivable (but not imperceivable) differences in subjects by balancing these characteristics between the two comparative groups. This is case matching.

Example of case-matching

It is the year 2002. Patients who happened to receive treatment A at a clinic in the year 2000 were predominantly female and younger, while those who received treatment B were mostly male and older. The investigator compares treatment A with treatment B by picking, for example, a female in the 30-40 year age category who received treatment A and a (harder-to-find) female in the same age category who happened to have received treatment B. The investigator does the same for females in the 50-60 year age category and in the 70-80 year age category, etc., and for males in the same age categories. The investigator now has a group who received treatment A that is evenly balanced by age and gender with a group who received treatment B, and he may proceed with computation of the study outcome.

Propensity Scoring

In a case-control study, subjects who received treatment A and those who received treatment B are chosen retrospectively to be matched according to age, gender, and any other relevant criteria that can be measured. In an analysis based on propensity scores, subjects in group A are matched with those subjects in group B who have the same propensity score, where the propensity score is the probability that a subject will be assigned to group B rather than group A based on a composite of observable determining characteristics [Joffe, 1999]. The study population is then divided into categories (usually quintiles) based on their propensity score and within each quintile the outcomes of individuals who received treatment A are compared with those received treatment B. Propensity score matching is based on two technical assumptions [Robinson, 2004]:

* **Assumption 1** (conditional independence assumption or CIA): there is a set X of covariates, observable to the researcher, such that after controlling for these covariates, the potential outcomes are independent of the treatment status. The CIA is crucial for correctly identifying the impact of the program, since it ensures that, although treated and untreated groups differ, these differences may be accounted for in order to reduce the selection bias. This allows the untreated units to be used to construct a counterfactual for the treatment group.

* **Assumption 2** (common support condition): for each value of X, there is a positive probability of being both treated and untreated. Then, a simple way of interpreting this assumption is the following: the proportion of treated and untreated individuals must be greater than zero for every possible value of X.

When these two assumptions are satisfied, the treatment assignment is said to be **strongly ignorable** [Robinson, 2004].

6.3.5 | Selection Bias in Subjects After Entering the Study

In a randomized controlled trial, subjects initially allocated to receive (say) treatment A might subsequently leave their assigned

6. Data Sources and Accounting for Uncertainty

treatment group and receive no treatment, an unplanned treatment, or switch to treatment B. In an intent-to-treat analysis, all subjects initially assigned to receive treatment A are included in the analysis of outcomes of group A. This ensures that the function of randomization – the control for selection bias – is preserved. A selection bias would be introduced if patients who left their assigned treatment group were not included in the analysis, since these patients were subject to some form of selection. The same intent-to-treat approach can be applied to retrospective studies.

6.4 Pharmacoeconomic Studies

6.4.1 Sensitivity Analysis

The sample decision analysis described earlier (see Chapter 3) contained an example of one-way sensitivity analysis. One-way sensitivity analysis is an example of simple sensitivity analysis, which is one of several general approaches.

Simple Sensitivity Analysis

In simple sensitivity analysis, one study variable is varied over the range of likely values, while all other variables are held constant. If the variables are independent, a series of one-way sen-

> **Example**
>
> A decision analytic DES model was built recently [Pradelli, 2012a] in order to compare the cost-effectiveness of two treatment alternatives for patients needing parenteral nutrition: use of parenteral omega-3 enriched emulsions or standard fat emulsions. A one-way analysis is applied on the base case scenario to study which parameters are most influential on final results. Given that the main conclusion of the base-case simulation is dominance (parenteral omega-3 vs. standard fat emulsion), it was chosen to explore the effect of parameter value estimates on total incremental costs (Figure 18) by a deterministic one-way analysis.

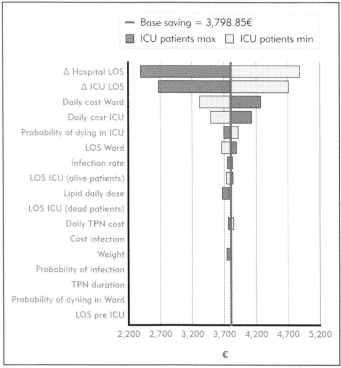

Figure 18. Example of a tornado diagram. The extremes of the 95%CI were selected as minimum and maximum values of parameters; for variables without such intervals, a ±20% variation is applied to baseline values.

sitivities is informative. In two-way sensitivity analysis, the effects of varying two variables simultaneously are computed. Similarly, in three-way sensitivity analysis, three variables are varied over their likely ranges of values at the same time. Two- and three-way sensitivity analyses are more appropriate when study variables interact. The calculations are performed using a computer program and the results displayed graphically.

Results of one-way analysis can be represented by a tornado diagrams, a special type of bar chart, where the data categories are listed vertically instead of the standard horizontal presenta-

6. Data Sources and Accounting for Uncertainty

tion, and the categories are ordered so that the largest bar appears at the top of the chart, the second largest appears second from the top, and so on. These graphs are so named because the final chart appears like a tornado (Figure 18).

Probabilistic Analysis

Instead of performing several one-way or multi-way analyses, it would be more desirable to perform an "every way" analysis, i.e., simultaneously vary all of the study variables throughout their ranges of likely values. A computer program can do this by starting with an imaginary cohort of, say, 1,000 patients and running them one by one through the decision tree, randomly assigning a likely value for the probability at each chance node.

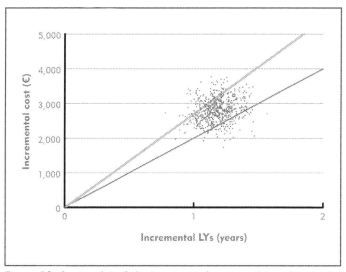

Figure 19. Scatterplot of the incremental costs and benefits on the cost-effectiveness plane elaborated by Eandi et al. [Eandi, 2010]. Black square indicates ICER in the base case while the slope of straight lines represents possible WTP (willingness to pay) thresholds (€20,000 and €27,000 for black and grey lines respectively). Number of points under the lines are simulated-patients within the threshold associated with each line (as shown in Figure 20).

A distribution of outcome values for the entire 1,000 patients can be thus calculated, and a mean and 95% confidence interval (95%CI) computed. When distributions for the values of chance node probabilities are known, the computer can take these into account (rather than assuming a uniform distribution within a range of values).

The patient-level, probabilistic simulation (also called Monte Carlo simulation) is performed by drawing parameter values from their probability distribution for each simulated individual, and allows to take into account two levels of uncertainty [Briggs, 2001]:

- the uncertainty on patient characteristics, which represents the effective heterogeneity among subjects;

- the uncertainty about model parameters, to represent the cognitive uncertainty on values derived from experimental measurements.

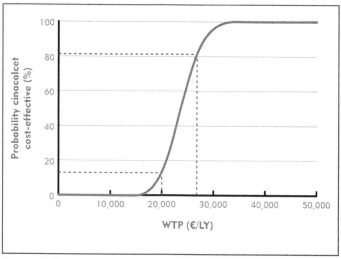

Figure 20. Cost-effectiveness acceptability curve elaborated from [Eandi, 2010]. Cinacalcet versus standard therapy has an estimated 13% or 82% probability of being cost-effective if the decision maker is willing to pay (WTP) up to 20,000€/LY or 27,000€/LY respectively.

6. Data Sources and Accounting for Uncertainty

In cost-effectiveness analysis, results of probabilistic analysis can be represented by a scatterplot: incremental costs and benefits are plotted on the cost-effectiveness plane and the grade of dispersion of the cloud of points can provide a visual indication of model stability (Figure 19).

Another indication of results reliability is given by the cost-effectiveness acceptability curves (CEAC) [Briggs, 2001] where the willingness to pay (WTP) for a unit benefit gained from a hypothetical decision-maker (i.e. the cost-effectiveness threshold considered as acceptable) is placed on the x-axis and the probability that an intervention is cost-effective compared with the alternative, given the observed data, on the y-axis (Figure 20).

Best and Worst Case Scenarios

This form of sensitivity analysis is more formally called **analysis of extremes**. A best-case estimate of cost effectiveness would combine the lower extreme estimate of costs and the upper extreme estimate of effectiveness. Similarly, a worst-case estimate would combine the upper extreme of costs and the lower extreme of effectiveness. Compared to a Monte Carlo simulation, this type of analysis is crude, but it is useful in some circumstances.

Threshold Analysis

Threshold analysis is a modification of one-way sensitivity analysis. Instead of a single variable being varied throughout its range of likely values, it is varied with the purpose of finding the threshold at which the decision alternatives have the same expected value. The threshold is also called the breakeven point.

6.5 Conclusions: Evaluating Pharmacoeconomic Studies

The established standard for assessing any published study is that sufficient information should be presented for a peer researcher to be able to repeat the study (and get the same answer). In the case of a cost-effectiveness analysis, this completely described in the text, and that all study variables and information sources be reported.

Many published cost-effectiveness analyses are black boxes that are difficult for the average reader to assess let alone reproduce; in such circumstances, the credibility of the researchers is important. Guidelines or checklists can be useful aids in assessing studies. Guidelines for evaluating pharmacoeconomic studies have been presented by university researchers [Anonymous, 1995], the Pharmaceutical Research and Manufacturers of America [Clemens, 1995], and state governments [Torrance, 1996]. In addition to these, criteria for assessing the conduct and reporting of various kinds of studies have been developed. The Users' Guides to the medical literature series published in *JAMA* includes articles on the assessment of economic analysis [Drummond, 1997], decision analysis [Richardson, 1995a; Richardson, 1995b; O'Brien, 1997; Naylor, 1996], health-related quality of life/outcomes research [Guyatt, 1997; Anonymous, 1995; Hartmaier, 1995], and systematic reviews [Oxman, 1994]. There are also published criteria for the reporting of clinical trials (CONSORT) [Moher, 1998] and for writing manuscripts of different types [International Committee of Medical Journal Editors, 1997].

6. Data Sources and Accounting for Uncertainty

REFERENCES

* Anonymous. Economic analysis of health care technology. A report on principles. Task Force on Principles for Economic Analysis of Health Care Technology. *Ann Intern Med* 1995; 123: 61-70

* Anonymous. Patient-Reported Outcomes Measurement (PROM) Group, 2012. Available at: http://phi.uhce.ox.ac.uk/home.php. (Latest access Oct 2012) [a]

* Anonymous. Pharmacoeconomics and outcomes: applications for patient care. Kansas City, MO: American College of Clinical Pharmacy, 1996

* Anonymous. PROQOLID, the Patient-Reported Outcome and Quality Of Life Instruments Database, 2012. Available at: http://www.proqolid.org. (Latest access Oct 2012) [b]

* ASSR. Agenzia Nazionale per i Servizi Sanitari Regionali. Ricoveri, personale e spesa delle aziende ospedaliere (2003). Available at: http://www.agenas.it/agenas_pdf/AO_2003.pdf [in Italian] (Latest access Oct 2012)

* ATS Committee on Proficiency Standards for Clinical Pulmonary Function Laboratories. ATS statement: guidelines for the six-minute walk test. *Am J Respir Crit Care Med* 2002; 166: 111-7. Available at: http://www.ncbi.nlm.nih.gov/pubmed/12091180. (Last accessed Oct 2012)

* Bergner M, Bobbitt RA, Carter WB, et al. The Sickness Impact Profile: development and final revision of a health status measure. *Med Care* 1981; 19: 787-805. Available at: http://www.ncbi.nlm.nih.gov/pubmed/7278416. (Last accessed Oct 2012)

* Briggs A. Handling uncertainty in economic evaluations and presenting the results. In: Drummond M, McGuire

A (eds.). Economic evaluation in health care. New York, NY: Oxford University Press, 2001; pp. 172-214

* Brooks R. EuroQol: the current state of play. *Health Policy* 1996; 37: 53-72. Available at: http://www.ncbi.nlm.nih.gov/pubmed/10158943. (Last accessed Oct 2012)

* Caldwell DM, Ades AE, Higgins JPT. Simultaneous comparison of multiple treatments: combining direct and indirect evidence. *BMJ* 2005; 331: 897-900

* Cavallo MC, Lazzaro C, Tabacchi M, et al. Cost of ICU in Italy. Results from an empirical study on a sample of 12 hospitals. *Minerva Anestesiol* 2001; 67: 41-53

* Chalmers I, Hetherington J, Elbourne D, et al. Materials and methods used in synthesizing evidence to evaluate the effects of care during pregnancy and childbirth. In: Chalmers I, Enkin M, Kerrse MJN (eds). Effective care in pregnancy and childbirdth. Col 1: Pregnancy. New York, NY: Oxford University Press, 1989; pp. 39-65

* Clemens K, Townsend R, Luscombe F, et al. Methodological and conduct principles for pharmacoeconornic research. Pharmaceutical Research and Manufacturers of America. *Pharmacoeconomics* 1995; 8: 69-74

* Department of Health. Guidance on the routine collection of Patient Reported Outcome Measures (PROMs). 2009. Available at: http://www.dh.gov.uk/en/Publicationsandstatistics/Publications/PublicationsPolicyAndGuidance/DH_092647. (Last accessed Oct 2012)

* Drummond MF, Richardson WS, O'Brien BJ, et al. Users' guides to the medical literature. XUI. How to use 'an article on economic analysis of clinical practice. A. Are the results of the study. Evidence based Medicine Working Group. *JAMA* 1997; 277: 1552-7

* Eandi M, Pradelli L, Iannazzo S, et al. Economic evaluation of cinacalcet in the treatment of secondary hyperparathyroidism in Italy. *Pharmacoeconomics* 2010; 28: 1041-54

- Eknoyan GLA. K/DOQI Clinical Practice Guidelines for Bone Metabolism and Disease in Chronic Kidney Disease. *Am J Kidney Dis* 2003; 42(Suppl 3): S1-S201

- Emery MP, Perrier LL, Acquadro C. Patient-Reported Outcome and Quality of Life Instruments Database (PROQOLID): Frequently asked questions. *Health and Quality of Life Outcomes* 2005; 3: 12. Available at: http://www.hqlo.com/content/3/1/12/abstract. (Last accessed Oct 2012)

- European Medicines Agency. Fourth report on the progress of the interaction with patients' and consumers' organizations (2010) and results/analysis of the degree of satisfaction of patients and consumers involved in EMA activities during 2010. 2011. Available at: http://www.ema.europa.eu/docs/en_GB/document_library/Other/2011/10/WC500115956.pdf. (Last accessed Oct 2012)

- European Medicines Agency. Plan for implementation of the pharmacovigilance legislation by the European Medicines Agency, 2012. Available at: http://www.ema.europa.eu/docs/en_GB/document_library/Other/2012/02/WC500121837.pdf. (Last accessed Oct 2012)

- European Medicines Agency. Rejection Paper on the Regulatory Guidance for the Use of Health Related Quality of Life (HRQL) Measures in the Evaluation of Medicinal Products. London: EMA, 2005. Available at: http://www.ema.europa.eu/docs/en_GB/document_library/Scientific_guideline/2009/09/WC500003637.pdf. (Last accessed Oct 2012)

- Farnik M. Instrument development and evaluation for patient-related outcomes assessments. *Patient Relat Outcome Meas* 2012; 3:1-7. Available at: http://www.dovepress.com/getfile.php?fileID=12205. (Last accessed Oct 2012)

- Fayers PM, Machin D. Quality of life: the assessment, analysis and interpretation of patient-reported outcomes. London: John Wiley & Sons, 2007

* Food and Drug Administration. Food and Drug Administration. Guidance for Indus-Patient-Reported Outcome Measures: Use in Medical Product Development to Support Labeling Claims. Rockville, MD: FDA, 2006. Available at: http://www.fda.gov/ohrms/dockets/98fr/06d-0044-gdl0001.pdf. (Last accessed Oct 2012)

* Food and Drug Administration. Food and Drug Administration. Guidance for Indus-Patient-Reported Outcome Measures: Use in Medical Product Development to Support Labeling Claims. Rockville, MD: FDA, 2009. Available at: http://www.fda.gov/downloads/Drugs/GuidanceComplianceRegulatoryInformation/Guidances/UCM071975.pdf. (Last accessed Oct 2012)

* Furlong WJ, Feeny DH, Torrance GW, et al. The Health Utilities Index (HUI) system for assessing health-related quality of life in clinical studies. *Ann Med* 2001; 33: 375-84

* GIVITI. Progetto Margherita. Rapporto 2007. Gruppo Italiano per la Valutazione degli Interventi in Terapia Intensiva (GIVITI), 2007 [in Italian]

* GIVITI. Progetto Margherita. Report 2009. Gruppo Italiano per la Valutazione degli Interventi in Terapia Intensiva (GIVIT), 2009 [in Italian]

* Glick H, Cook J, Kinosian B, et al. Costs and effects of enalapril therapy in patients with symptomatic heart failure. An economic analysis of the studies of the left ventricular dysfunction (SOLVD) treatment trial. *J Cardiac Failure* 1995; 1: 371-9

* Gupchup GV, Wolfgang AP, Thomas J 3rd. Reliability and validity of the Asthma Quality of Life Questionnaire-marks in a sample of adult asthmatic patients in the United States. *Clin Ther* 1997; 19: 1116-25

* Guyatt G, Naylor CD, Juniper E, et al. Users' guides to the medical literature. XII. How to use articles about health-related quality of life. Evidence-Based Medicine Working Group. *JAMA* 1997; 277: 1232-7

106

* Hartmaier SL, Santanello NC, Epstein RS, et al. Development of a brief 24-hour migraine-specific quality of life questionnaire. *Headache* 1995; 35: 320-9

* Haynes RB, McKibbon KA, Kanani R. Systematic review of randomised trials of interventions to assist patients to follow prescriptions for medications. *Lancet* 1996; 348: 383-6

* Henshaw SK. Unintended pregnancy in the United States. *Fam Plann Perspect* 1998; 30: 24-9

* Hilleman DE, Heineman SM, Foral PA. Pharmacoeconomic assessment of HMG-CoA reductase inhibitor therapy: an analysis based on the CURVES study. *Pharmacotherapy* 2000; 20: 819-22

* Hunt SM, McKenna SP, McEwen J, et al. A quantitative approach to perceived health status: a validation study. *J Epidemiol Community Health* 1980; 34: 281-6. Available at: http://www.ncbi.nlm.nih.gov/pubmed/7241028. (Last accessed Oct 2012)

* International Committee of Medical Journal Editors. Uniform Requirements for Manuscripts Submitted to Biomedical Journals. *JAMA* 1997; 277: 927-34

* Jackowski D, Guyatt G. A guide to health measurement. *Clin Orthop Relat Res* 2003; 413: 80-9

* Jacobson SH, Hall SN, Swisher JR. Discrete event simulation of health care systems, patient flow: reducing delay in healthcare delivery (Ed. Hall RW). *International Series in Operations Research & Management Science* 2006; 91: 211-52

* Joffe MM, Rosenbaum PR. Invited commentary: propensity scores. *Am J Epidemiol* 1999; 150: 327-33

* Johnson RE, Hornbrook MC, Hooker RS, et al. Analysis of the costs of NSAID-associated gastropathy. Experience in a US health maintenance organisation. *Pharmacoeconomics* 1997; 12: 76-88

* Jones R, Coyne K, Wiklund I. The gastro-oesophageal reflux disease impact scale: a patient management tool for primary care. *Aliment Pharmacol Ther* 2007; 25: 1451-9

* Khanna D, Tsevat J. Health-related quality of life--an introduction. *The American Journal of Managed Care* 2007; 13 (Suppl 9): S218-23. Available at: https://myvpn.med.utah.edu/pubmed/,DanaInfo=www.ncbi.nlm.nih.gov+18095785. (Last accessed Oct 2012)

* King MT. A point of minimal important difference (MID): a critique of terminology and methods. *Expert Rev Pharmacoecon Outcomes Res* 2011; 11:171-84. Available at: http://www.ncbi.nlm.nih.gov/pubmed/21476819. (Last accessed Oct 2012)

* La Torre G. Applied epidemiology and biostatistics. Torino: SEEd, 2010

* Lachin JM. Statistical properties of randomization in clinical trials. *Control Clin Trials* 1988; 9: 289-311

* Marciante KD, Gardner JS, Veenstra DL, et al. Modeling the cost and outcomes of pharmacist-prescribed emergency contraception. *Am J Public Health* 2001; 91: 1443-5

* Mauskopf JA, Sullivan SD, Annemans L, et al.Principles of Good Practice for Budget Impact Analysis: Report of the ISPOR Task Force on Good Research Practices-Budget Impact Analysis. *Value in Health* 2007; 10: 336-47

* Messa P, Macário F, Yaqoob M, The OPTIMA Study: assessing a new cinacalcet (Sensipar/Mimpara) treatment algorithm for secondary hyperparathyroidism. *Clin J Am Soc Nephrol* 2008; 3: 36-45

* Miller JH, Page SE. Complex adaptive systems: an introduction to computational models of social life (Princeton Studies in Complexity). Princeton: Princeton University Press, 2007

* Moher D. CONSORT: an evolving tool to help improve the quality of reports of randomized controlled trials.

108

Consolidated Standards of Reporting Trials. *JAMA* 1998; 279: 489-91

* Murray CJ, Lopez AD. Global mortality, disability, and the contribution of risk factors: Global Burden of Disease Study. *Lancet* 1997; 349: 1436-42

* Naylor CD, Guyatt GH. Users' guides to the medical literature. X. How to use an article reporting variations in the outcomes of health services. The Evidence-Based Medicine Working Group. *JAMA* 1996; 275: 554-8

* Niazi M, Hussain A. Agent-based computing from multi-agent systems to agent-based models: a visual survey. *Scientometrics* 2011; 89: 479-99

* O'Brien BJ, Heyland D, Richardson WS, et al. Users guides to the medical literature. XIII. How to use an article on economic analysts of clinical practice. B. What are the results and will they help me in caring for my patients? Evidence-Based Medicine Working Group. *JAMA* 1997; 277: 1802-6

* OECD. Health at a Glance 2011. OECD Indicators. OECD Publishing, 2011. Available at: http://www.oecd.org/health/healthpoliciesanddata/healthataglance2011.htm. (Last accessed Oct 2012)

* Orsi GB, Di Stefano L, Noah N. Hospital-acquired, laboratory-confirmed bloodstream infection: Increased hospital stay and direct costs. *Infect Control Hosp Epidemiol* 2002; 23: 190-7

* Oxman AD, Cook OJ, Guyatt GH. Users' guides to the medical literature. VI. How to use an overview. Evidence-Based Medicine Working Group. *JAMA* 1994; 272: 1367-71

* Patrick DL, Burke LB, Gwaltney CJ, et al. Content Validity—Establishing and Reporting the Evidence in Newly Developed Patient-Reported Outcomes (PRO) Instruments for Medical Product Evaluation: ISPOR PRO Good Research Practices Task Force Report: Part 1—Eliciting

Concepts for a New PRO Instrument. *Value in Health* 2011; 14: 967-77. Available at: http://www.valuein-healthjournal.com/article/S1098-3015(11)03323-7/abstract. (Last accessed Oct 2012) [a]

❋ Patrick DL, Burke LB, Gwaltney CJ, et al. Content Validity—Establishing and Reporting the Evidence in Newly Developed Patient-Reported Outcomes (PRO) Instruments for Medical Product Evaluation: ISPOR PRO Good Research Practices Task Force Report: Part 2—Assessing Respondent Understanding. *Value in Health* 2011; 14: 978-88 [b]

❋ Patrick DL, Burke LB, Powers JH, et al. Patient-Reported Outcomes to Support Medical Product Labeling Claims: FDA Perspective. *Value in Health* 2007; 10(s2): S125-S137. Available at: http://dx.doi.org/10.1111/j.1524-4733.2007.00275.x. (Last accessed Oct 2012)

❋ Petitti DB. Meta-analysis, decision analysis, and cost effectiveness analysis. methods for quantitatitive synthesis in medicine. Monographs in epidemiology and biostatistics. Volume 24. New York, NY: Oxford University Press, 1994

❋ Pignone M, Phillips C, Mulrow C. Use of lipid lowering drugs for primary prevention of coronary heart disease: meta-analysis of randomized trials. *BMJ* 2000; 321: 983-6

❋ Poolman RW, Swiontkowski MF, Fairbank JCT, et al. Outcome Instruments: Rationale for Their Use. *J Bone Joint Surg Am* 2009; 91(Suppl 3): 41-9. Available at: http://www.ncbi.nlm.nih.gov/pmc/articles/PMC2669748/. (Last accessed Oct 2012)

❋ Poret AW, Neslusan C, Ricci J, et al. Retrospective analysis of the health care costs of bupropion sustained release in comparison with other antidepressants. *Value in Health* 2001; 4: 362-9

110

* Pradelli L, Eandi M, Povero M, et al. Cost-effectiveness of supplemental n-3 in total parenteral nutrition therapy in the Italian, French, German and UK context: a discrete event simulation model. *Value in Health* 2012; 15: A539 [a]

* Pradelli L, Iannazzo S, Zaniolo O, et al. Effectiveness and cost-effectiveness of supplemental glutamine dipeptide in total parenteral nutrition therapy for critically ill patients: a discrete event simulation model based on Italian data. *Int J Technol Assess* 2012; 28: 22-8 [b]

* Reichenberg K, Broberg AG. Quality of life in childhood asthma: use of the Paediatric Asthma Quality of Life Questionnaire in a Swedish sample of children 7 to 9 years old. *Acta Paediatr* 2000; 89: 989-95

* Revicki D, Hays RD, Cella D, et al. Recommended methods for determining responsiveness and minimally important differences for patient-reported outcomes. *J Clin Epidemiol* 2008; 61: 102-9

* Richardson WS, Detsky AS. Users' guides to the medical literature. VII. How to use a clinical decision analysis. A. Are the results of the study valid? Evidence-Based Medicine Working Group. *JAMA* 1995; 273: 1292-5 [a]

* Richardson WS, Detsky AS. Users' guides to the medical literature. VII. How to use a clinical decision analysis. B. What are the results and will they help me in caring for my patients? Evidence Based Medicine Working Group. *JAMA* 1995; 273: 1610 3 [b]

* Robinson S. Simulation. The practice of model development and use. London: Wiley, 2004

* Rosenbaum P, Rubin D. The central role of the propensity score in observational studies for causal effects. *Biometrika* 1983; 70: 41-55

❋ Roter DL, Hall JA, Merisca R, et al. Effectiveness of inter-ventions to improve patient compliance: a meta- analysis. *Med Care* 1998; 36: 138-61

❋ Rothman ML, Beltran P, Cappelleri JC, et al. Patient-Reported Outcomes: Conceptual Issues. *Value in Health* 2007; 10(S2): S66-S75. Available at: http://www.valuein-healthjournal.com/article/S1098-3015(10)60631-6/ab-stract. (Last accessed Oct 2012)

❋ Rubinstein E, Kaksa A, Ho Y, et al. Use of Pro Analysis in Health Technology Assessments. In: The ISPOR Out-comes Research Digest. Washington, DC: ViH, 2012:PIH 55. Available at: http://www.ispor.org/research_pdfs/40/ pdffiles/PIH55.pdf. (Last accessed Oct 2012)

❋ Squires A, Bruyneel L, Aiken LH, et al. Cross-cultural evaluation of the relevance of the HCAHPS survey in five European countries. *Int J Qual Health Care* 2012; 24: 470-5

❋ Terwee CB, Bot SDM, de Boer MR, et al. Quality criteria were proposed for measurement properties of health status questionnaires. *J Clin Epidemiol* 2007; 600: 34-42

❋ Torrance GW, Blaker D, Detsky A, et al. Canadian guide-lines for economic evaluation of pharmaceuticals. Cana-dian Collaborative Workshop for Pharmacoeconomics. *Pharmacoeconomics* 1996; 9: 535-59

❋ Trotti A, Colevas AD, Setser A, et al. Patient-reported outcomes and the evolution of adverse event reporting in oncology. *J Clin Oncol* 2007; 25: 5121-7. Available at: https://myvpn.med.utah.edu/pubmed/,DanaInfo=www. ncbi.nlm.nih.gov+17991931. (Last accessed Oct 2012)

❋ van Hout BA, Wielink G, Bonsel GJ, et al. Effects of ACE inhibitors on heart failure in The Netherlands: a phar-macoeconomic model. *Pharmacoeconomics* 1993; 3: 387-97

❋ Ware JE Jr, Sherbourne CD. The MOS 36-item short-form health survey (SF-36). I. Conceptual framework and item selection. *Med Care* 1992; 30: 473-83. Available at: http://www.ncbi.nlm.nih.gov/pubmed/1593914. (Last accessed Oct 2012)

* Wilson IB, Cleary PD. Linking clinical variables with health-related quality of life. A conceptual model of patient outcomes. *JAMA* 1995; 273: 59-65

* World Health Organization. WHO definition of Health. 1948. Available at: http://www.who.int/about/definition/en/print.html. (Last accessed Oct 2012)

* Zaniolo O, Bettoncelli G, Bosio G, et al. Ricerca assistenza e programmazione: dall'audit clinico al modello di impatto sul budget nella BPCO. *Farmeconomia e percorsi terapeutici* 2010; 11: 121-35 [in Italian]

GLOSSARY

Average cost

Total costs of a treatment or programme divided by total quantity of treatment units provided (see also "Marginal cost").

Budget impact analysis (BIA)

A tool to predict the potential financial impact of the adoption and diffusion of a new technology into a health care system with finite resources.

Consequence

In health economics, the effects, outputs, or outcomes of the program or drug therapy of interest.

Cost

In health economics, the value of the resources consumed by a program or drug therapy of interest.

Cost-benefit analysis (CBA)

Type of analysis that measures costs and benefits in pecuniary units and computes a net monetary gain/loss or a cost-benefit ratio.

Cost-effectiveness analysis (CEA)

CEA has been defined by NICE as an economic study design in which consequences of different interventions are measured using a single outcome, usually in "natural" units (for example, life-years gained, deaths avoided, heart attacks avoided, or cases detected), and the interventions are compared in terms of cost per unit of effectiveness.

Cost-effectiveness ratio (ICER)

The ratio of the change in costs of a therapeutic intervention (compared to the alternative, such as doing nothing or using the best available alternative treatment) to the change in effects of the intervention.

Cost-minimization analysis (CMA)

Type of analysis that finds the least costly programme among those shown or assumed to be of equal benefit.

Cost-utility analysis (CUA)

Type of analysis that measures benefits in utility-weighted life-years (QALYs); computes a cost per utility-measure ratio for comparison between programmes.

Decision tree

A framework for representing alternatives for use in decision analysis.

Defined daily dose (DDD)

The average maintenance dose for the clinical indication of a drug in adult patients.

Direct cost

The direct cost of an illness to society is the cost of providing all of the health care services to treat it, including the costs of medicines, physician visits, emergency room visits, and hospitalizations due to the disease.

116

Disability adjusted life years (DALYs)

The sum of years of potential life lost due to premature mortality and the years of productive life lost due to disability.

Economic evaluation

An analysis that evaluates the costs and consequences of heath technologies.

Effectiveness

The extent to which a drug achieves its intended effect in the usual clinical setting.

Efficacy

The extent to which a drug has the ability to bring about its intended effect under ideal circumstances, such as in a randomized clinical trial.

Equity

Fairness in the allocation of resources or treatments among different individuals or groups.

Health maintenance organization (HMO)

Managed care plan that offers prepaid comprehensive healthcare coverage, minimal copay and coinsurance, and usually case management to those enrolled in the plan.

Health technology assessment (HTA)

According to the European network for Health Technology Assessment, it is «a multidisciplinary process that summarizes information about the medical, social, economic and ethical issues related to the use of a health technology in a systematic, transparent, unbiased, robust manner».

Health-related quality of life (HR-QOL)

A composite measure of the individual's physical health or biologic functioning, emotional or psychological state, level of independence, social relationships, and environmental forces.

Incremental cost

The increased cost of one treatment program relative to an alternative.

Indirect cost

The indirect cost of an illness to society is the value of the productivity lost when the disease prevents people from working.

Indirect cost

The value of the productivity loss resulting from an illness.

Intangible cost

The value of psychosocial effects such as pain and suffering.

Marginal cost

Change in total cost that results from the production of an additional unit.

Markov model

A statistical representation of recurrent events over time that can be incorporated into decision analysis.

Meta-analysis

A systematic method that uses statistical techniques for combining results from different studies to obtain a quantitative estimate of the overall effect of a particular intervention or variable on a defined outcome.

118

Monte Carlo simulation

A statistical technique in which a large quantity of randomly generated numbers are studied using a probabilistic model to find an approximate solution to a numerical problem that would be difficult to solve by other methods.

Mortality cost

The cost incurred due to death.

Opportunity cost

The value of all costs in an alternative use.

Outcomes research

Studies that attempt to identify, measure, and evaluate the results of healthcare services.

Overhead cost

The cost of providing space, power, administrative services, etc.

Patient reported outcome (PRO)

According to the Food and Drug Administration (FDA): «A type of data measuring any aspect of a patient's health status that comes directly from the patient». According to the European Medicines Agency: «Any outcome directly evaluated by the patient and based on patient's perception of a disease and its treatment(s)».

Pharmacoeconomics

A social science concerned with the description and analysis of the costs of pharmaceutical products and services and their impact on individuals, health care systems, and society.

Quality of life (QOL)

In general, a broad-ranging concept that describes the degree of well being impacted by many factors such as environment, family, work, social status, or health status. In health care, quality of life is often regarded in terms of how it is negatively affected by an individual's health.

Quality-adjusted life year (QALY)

A common measure of health improvement used in CUA: combines mortality and QOL gains (outcome of a treatment measured as the number of years of life saved, adjusted for quality).

Sensitivity analysis

A process through which the robustness of an economic model is assessed by examining the changes in results of the analysis when key variables are varied over a specific range.

Systematic review

A critical assessment and evaluation of all research studies that address a particular clinical issue. It can include a meta-analysis (quantitative pooling of data, see).

Willingness to pay (WTP)

The maximum amount of money that an individual is prepared to give up to ensure that a proposed health care measure is undertaken.

AUTHORS

Anke-Peggy Holtorf, PhD, MBA

Dr. Holtorf is the founder of the Health Outcomes Strategies, GmbH based in Basel, Switzerland. Her areas of expertise include decision making on health care products, outcomes research and health economics, health technology assessment processes, payer interactions, product/service synergies, and in summary, value based market access strategies. She has served as visiting faculty at the University of Utah between 2006 and 2007 and remains adjunct assistant professor in the Pharmacotherapy Outcomes Research Center at the University of Utah College of Pharmacy, where she in addition to her academic contributions participated as investigator in a variety of outcomes studies. She has published broadly, among others on subjects of evidence based decision making and quality control in healthcare. Next to serving as evaluator for health care research proposals the European Commission, Dr. Holtorf is member of the Health Technology Assessment international Association (HTAi) and the International Society of Pharmacoeconomics and Outcomes Research (ISPOR) where she is engaged in the Health Technology Assessment working groups for pharmaceuticals, medical devices and diagnostics and in the Personalized Medicine workgroup. She has also been appointed as evaluator at the EU-commission. Dr. Holtorf obtained her PhD from the University of Marburg (Germany) and her MBA from the University of Birmingham (United Kingdom). She looks back on over 20 years of experience in the pharmaceutical and chemical industry in research and marketing with global responsibilities. Among others, she was responsible for the global Disease Management activities and strategy of Novartis Pharma, AG.

Between 2000 and 2004, Dr. Holtorf managed the biotech business unit of a midsized Swiss chemical company and held a seat in the executive committee.

Ceri J. Phillips, BSc(Econ), MSc(Econ), PhD

Ceri Phillips is Professor of Health Economics at Swansea University Centre for Health Economics and Head of Research at the College of Human and Health Sciences, Swansea University, Wales. He is a non-executive member of Abertawe Bro Morgannwg Health Board and a member of the Bevan Commission, established by the Welsh Minister of Health and Social Services on the 60th anniversary of the NHS to advise and oversee the new configuration and structure of NHS Wales. He is also a member of the 1000 Lives+ Programme Board and the Management Board of the NICE Collaborating Centre for Cancer and has recently been a member of NICE Programme Development Groups on a range of public health issues. Up until November 2011 he was the health economics member of the All Wales Medicines Strategy Group (AWMSG), which advises the Welsh Minster of Health and Social Services on matters relating to prescribing decisions and medicines management, and was the Vice Chair of its New Medicines Group, which appraises all eligible new, licensed medicines, available for use in the NHS, and which makes recommendations to AWMSG. He has undertaken commissioned work on the evaluation of programmes and interventions for a range of organisations, including the World Health Organisation, Welsh Government, Department of Health, Department of Work and Pensions and a range of health and social care authorities and pharmaceutical companies. He has published extensively in the field of health economics, health and social policy, with over 140 books and journal articles.

Lorenzo Pradelli, MD

Lorenzo Pradelli is medical director at AdRes Health Economics and Outcomes Research srl, Torino, Italy. He is in charge

122

of the design, development and management of pharmaco-economic researches, with particular reference to the medical and scientific aspects. He is member of the scientific board of *Farmeconomia. Health economics and therapeutic pathways*, published by SEEd, and he is editor in chief of the monographic journal *Profili in Farmacoeconomia*. He's author and co-author of more than 30 articles on pharmacoeconomics, including original scientific papers in peer-reviewed journals, oral communications and poster presentations at national and international congresses. Dr. Pradelli is member of the International Society for Pharmacoeconomics and Outcomes Research (ISPOR) and the Italian Society for the study of Drug Economics and Ethics and Therapeutic Intervention (SIFEIT).

Albert Wertheimer, PhD, MBA

Albert Wertheimer is a professor of pharmacy economics at the School of Pharmacy, Temple University, Philadelphia, PA, USA, where has been since 2000. Previously, he was a professor at the University of Minnesota, Dean at the Philadelphia College of Pharmacy, Director of Health Outcomes Management at Merck and Company, and a vice president at First Health, a pharmacy benefit management (PBM) firm. He received a Bachelor of Pharmacy degree from the University of Buffalo; a Masters of Business Administration from the State University of New York at Buffalo, and a PhD degree from Purdue University. He was also a post-doctoral fellow at the Department of Social Medicine at St. Thomas' Hospital Medical School of the University of London (UK). He is the author or co-author of 31 books, 410 articles in scientific and professional journals and 30 book chapters. He has directed 85 Ph.D. students and a similar number of Masters degree students. Professor Wertheimer has consulted or lectured in over 60 countries. He holds visiting or adjunct professorships at Universities in Taiwan, Turkey, China, Mexico, Malaysia, among others. He is the editor of the quarterly journal, *Journal of Pharmaceutical Health Services Research*, published by Wiley-Blackwell. He has been the recipient of numerous international awards such as a Scheele Laureate from the Swedish Academy of Pharmaceutical Sciences, Fellowship in the Mexican Academy of Pharmaceutical Sciences, the Andre Bedat Award from the International Pharmacy Federation (FIP), research achievement award from the American Pharmacists Association, and Fellowship from the American Association of Pharmaceutical Scientists.

Dr. Wertheimer maintains an active consulting practice where he assists pharmaceutical companies, governmental and international agencies, professional societies and other clients. He lives near Philadelphia, Pennsylvania, USA.

Acknowledgements

A special thank to **Antonio Aliano**, **Marco Bellone**, **Massimiliano Povero** and **Orietta Zaniolo** (AdRes Health Economics and Outcomes Research srl, Torino, Italy) for their valuable assistance in the writing and data collection processes.